THE GREAT
COMMANDERS

THE GREAT

COMMANDERS

Phil Grabsky

ALEXANDER · CAESAR · NELSON · NAPOLEON · GRANT · ZHUKOV

Foreword by David G Chandler

THE HISTORY CHANNEL

VIEWER BOOKS

This is a Viewer Book
Published by TV Books, Inc.

All rights reserved under International and Pan-American
copyright conventions.

Published in the United States by TV Books, Inc., New York.
Distributed to the trade by Penguin USA, New York.

First published in Great Britain in 1993 by Boxtree Limited

© Phil Grabsky 1993

Viewer Books
TV Books, Inc.
1995 Broadway
New York, NY 10023

A CIP catalog entry for this book is available from the Library of Congress.

ISBN 1-57500-003-2

Title page: Soviet tanks in Berlin, battened down against counter-attack.

CONTENTS

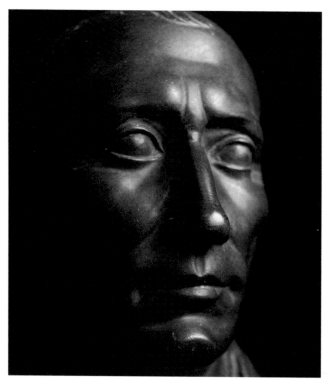

Bust of Julius Caesar from the Museo della Civilta, Romana

To My Parents

Foreword

Generalship is the highest form of military leadership. The correct exercise of command in war is one vital requirement for the achievement of success – and, in the event of defeat, for retrieving or at least minimizing the effects of failure. Of the many senior soldiers and sailors entrusted with high command in the wars of recorded history, only a very few ever aspired to the title of 'Great Captains'. Even fewer receive the accolade in their own lifetimes, as its conferment normally needs the confirmation of posterity when all the dust has settled and a reasonably objective assessment has emerged.

It is common practice to speak of the 'art and science of war'. The scientific elements of warfare change constantly as new weaponry, methods of communication and transportation become available. Many aspects of the art of war – which includes generalship – remain much the same, generation after generation, or at least retain clearly discernible characteristics in common – as this study of the great commanders will reveal.

Everyone interested in military and naval history will have his or her favourite commanders. Some names will probably figure on many lists – Alexander the Great, Caesar and Napoleon, for instance, exert a timeless fascination. Few lists of great sailors would exclude Nelson. All of these great names are treated below. Thereafter it is a matter for personal preference and judgement. To complete his personal list, Phil Grabsky has added Grant and Zhukov to represent the more recent period – and with good reason as both were very notable commanders in their respective centuries and generations. No doubt many readers would have selected other names for inclusion, as over the millennia of recorded history there are several dozen soldiers and sailors of sufficient stature to merit consideration for a work such as this.

Napoleon described his preferred list of great soldiers down to his own time as follows:

> Peruse again and again the campaigns of Alexander, Hannibal, Caesar, Gustavus Adolphus, Turenne, Eugene and Frederick. Model yourself upon them. This is the only means of becoming a great captain, and of acquiring the secret art of war . . . .

But Phil Grabsky is as entitled intellectually to his view of the great military figures of the past as Napoleon was to his. He has chosen a Macedonian, a Roman, an Englishman, a Corsican, an American and a Russian – and thus has cast his net pretty wide in terms of nationality. Military genius observes no boundaries of time, race, country or creed, and History (as Professor Geyl remarked in his book *Napoleon: For and Against* in 1945) is indeed '...an argument without end'. Therein lies much of the subject's fascination for soldiers, sailors and laypersons alike.

In 1939, on the eve of the Second World War, General (later Field-Marshal) Sir Archibald Wavell enumerated his views on the essentials of generalship in a series of lectures delivered at Cambridge University. The first requisite quality he defined as 'robustness, the ability to stand the shocks of war'. Warfare in all ages has been a rough business, the realm of the unexpected, and subject to what Clausewitz (the great 19th century military philosopher) termed 'friction'. As Wavell stressed, a commander's mind must be as hardy as his body: 'All material of war, including the general, must have a certain solidity, a high margin over the normal breaking strain.'

From Wavell and other sources it is possible to compile a non-exclusive working list of qualities required in a successful commander. As has already been mentioned in an earlier paragraph, the basic attributes needed in a general are little different today from what was required in the times of Alexander or Napoleon. Boldness –

Alexander riding his horse Bucephalus.

which Wavell connotes with what Napoleon called 'luck' – is clearly a major requirement. It must not of course be carried as far as fool-hardiness, but be based upon the careful calculation of risk. 'A bold general may be lucky, but no general can be lucky unless he is bold.' All the commanders described in this book are notable for their boldness.

A commander must also be able to inspire confidence in his subordinates. This may be easy enough when all is going well, but the acid test comes when everything appears to be going badly, and disaster seems to be in the making. The possession of a 'gallant heart in adversity' is a vital attribute.

This is closely connected to the possession of courage – both physical and moral. All men feel fear in war, but it must be come to terms with and not allowed to exercise a debilitating effect. Moral courage is probably the more difficult of the two to acquire – the ability to stand up to intense pressures and always aspire to do that which is right.

A good general or admiral must also have a developed ability to judge character, and be adept at choosing the right man for the job in hand. He must be tough – even a trifle callous – when it comes to removing inadequate subordinates. It is possible for him to be over-courteous and too considerate – perhaps Robert E. Lee, General Grant's great adversary, is a good example – but he should always be courteous.

Needless to say a commander must be the very embodiment of energy, drive and the will to win. This is closely linked to the ability to arouse and retain confidence already noted. He must have a large body of professional knowledge of all aspects of the martial trade, and constantly add to it and keep it under regular review. The quality of sound common sense needs to be much to the fore – linked to clarity of thought, particularly when the evaluation of intelligence information is concerned. A successful general must also be imaginative – but not to the extent of permitting his imagination to run away with him, which might well lead to dangerous miscalculations. He must also cultivate a sense of presence, or charisma, and develop a power to communicate his orders and ideas: Alexander, Napoleon and Nelson excelled in this respect. And, perhaps above all, he must evince a high degree of interest in, and real knowledge about, his men as human beings. This must not become sentimentality, for in time of war he will have to give orders inevitably involving the loss of many lives and the wounding of many more – but care for the welfare of his officers and men is a vital requisite for they are indispensable to any achievement to which he may hope to aspire.

There are several types of senior commander. The fighting-general is the most common image evoked, but others include the soldier-diplomat, the trainer of troops, the morale-builder, the coordinator of allies and the dedicated higher staff-officer. A general may undertake several of these roles in his career for none are exclusive, but the average commander is unlikely to shine in more than two. The great commander, however, has to excel in all categories if he is to be indeed a general or an admiral 'for all seasons'.

The requirements of a good general were described by the Greek philosopher, Socrates, in c. 400 BC:

> The general must know how to get his men their rations and every other
> kind of stores needed for war. He must have imagination to originate plans,
> practical sense, and energy to carry them through. He must be observant,
> untiring, shrewd, kindly and cruel, simple and crafty; a watchman and soldier;
> lavish and miserly; generous yet tight-fisted; both rash and conservative.
> All these and other qualities, natural and acquired, he must have. He should also,
> as a matter of course, know his tactics; for a disorderly mob is no more an army
> than a heap of building materials is a house.

This passage is almost as relevant today as in the period when it was composed. The essentials of generalship and high command are unchanging. In 1804 Napoleon was asked for his view of what went to make a successful commander. He listed concentration of force, activity of body and mind, and a firm resolve to perish gloriously. 'These are the three principles of the military art that have disposed luck in my favour in all my operations. Death is nothing, but to live defeated is to die every day.'

DAVID G. CHANDLER
1993

Introduction

It is an unhappy fact that the development of civilization has been shaped by war. With justification, Winston Churchill referred to battles as the 'punctuation marks on the pages of secular history', and the outcome of these encounters is often in the hands of only a few individuals. The intention of this book, and the Channel Four television series, is to look at six such figures, generally held to be 'great' commanders, who, as a result of their exceptional military abilities, changed the course of history.

There can be no league table of military commanders – each must be seen in the context of his (and, on rare occasions, her) society. The most one can hope to achieve when considering them collectively is to understand the circumstances in which they lived, the processes by which they made their decisions, and the effects those actions had. From each we can then seek to learn something of relevance. In many ways, in our day-to-day lives, we are all either a commander or commanded. The lessons that can be drawn from examining six very different military leaders are as illuminating to a businessperson, a sportsperson or a politician as they are to a soldier or sailor.

Accepting that there can be no realistic and agreed hierarchy of the 'greatest' commanders in history, how were the six chosen for this book and the series? Certainly the following are generally considered to be six of the greatest by both historians and soldiers. And military academies continue to look to them for inspiration. But there have been many thousands of excellent commanders in history. My first objective was to paint a broad picture on a canvas that stretched from antiquity through to the twentieth-century. Is there, I wondered, any possible relationship between command two thousand years ago and today? Is there any validity in the idea that while the science of war is forever changing, the art of war is a constant?

Clearly, several of the commanders in this book benefitted from their ability to be the first and the best at exploiting new technological developments. It was my intention, therefore, to follow the development from the 'commander-king' (such as

Red Army Cavalry poster.

Alexander) to the 'commander-subordinate' (such as Zhukov). In this way it was possible to see that although the environment in which a military commander works has altered enormously, the 'great' commanders are those who understand the changes and excel in spite – or because – of them.

My choice has provoked stimulating debate. I hope it will continue to do so. It is not intended as a statement of conclusive fact. Every age and epoch produces its great leaders – and only some of them are military.

All six of these commanders caused thousands, sometimes hundreds of thousands, of fatal casualties. Perhaps to call them 'great' is too generous and in both book and television series I have tried not to forget that the men and women who died were much more than mere numbers. However, although wars are not in themselves glorious, in their brutality and despair, glory – and genius – can be found.

Acknowledgments

I would like to thank a number of people who were instrumental in the writing of this book: Michael Attwell at Channel 4, without whose encouragement and 'command' there would have been no TV series; Sandy Holton and Susanna Yager at C4 Publishing; the many others at Channel 4 (UK) and A&E (USA), Ambrose Video (USA), The History Channel (USA), SBS (Australia) and Sovtelexport (Russia), who were also involved in the television series; Susanna Wadeson and Sarah Mahaffy at Boxtree (UK), TV Books, Inc (USA); David Chandler and all those I consulted – especially Michael Whitby, Peter Connolly, Simon James, Colin White, Tom Pocock, Jay Luvaas, Carol Reardon, Otto Chaney, Richard Lakowski and Tony Le Tissier – their expertise and selflessness were invaluable. Within my own company, Seventh Art Productions, I would like to give particular credit to my researchers David Coward and Ben Goold. Above all, I wish to thank Amanda Wilkie, my production manager, without whom this project would not have been made.

ΓΝΩΣΙΣ ΕΠΟΗΣΕΝ

CHAPTER ONE

ALEXANDER THE GREAT

'There has never been another man in all the world, who by his own hand succeeded in so many brilliant enterprises.' (Arrian)

Alexander the Great is considered the greatest of all history's commanders. Many have tried to emulate him – and failed. Men like Caesar and Napoleon, who honoured no-one but themselves, bowed before his memory.

An important element of great command is the ability to create and propagate one's own legend. Alexander of Macedon knew this and employed historians to record his deeds and actions. From their words – copied and filtered through the centuries – we have a record of the world's first great conqueror, whose ambition and success have inspired military commanders through the centuries. The energy and determination of this young man, at the head of a highly trained and motivated army, fuelled a relentless expansion that conquered lands from Greece to India. It was a vast empire at a time when communication travelled no faster than a horse. And it was an empire won through military genius.

Alexander's personal and inspirational leadership made his soldiers believe in him as an all-conquering, invincible hero. He earned their affection to such an extent that they would rather die than disgrace his name. In lands and against peoples that none of them, indeed none of their race, had seen before, his men were never to suffer the humiliation of defeat.

Alexander's decision not only to attempt to conquer the known world but also to reveal his achievements to all means that there may be serious distortions in the historical evidence. But even when cautious of legend, one can still understand why many see Alexander as the founding father of great military command.

He was born in 356 BC, the son of King Philip II of Macedonia. This land of mountains and forests, lying just to the north of Greece, was populated with peasants

Pebble mosaic of a deer hunt from the palace at Pella, capital of the Macedonian empire.

controlled by nobles and cattle barons. Above them all sat Philip, an 'absolute autocrat, commander, and master of everybody and everything'. This Macedonian king was highly ambitious and by improving and exploiting his armed forces had substantially extended his territorial borders. Philip bore many scars of battle but was always willing to pay this price if victory was the outcome.

Philip's first wife died while giving birth to a daughter and his second wife also died young. Not until Philip married the manipulative, passionate Olympias did he succeed in siring the son he wanted. Alexander was everything Philip had wished for – handsome, healthy and intelligent. Even as a boy he seemed predisposed towards leadership. The Greek historian Plutarch recounted a story in which Alexander, during his father's absence on campaign, received ambassadors from the Persian court. After winning them over with his welcome, he impressed them with his perceptive questions on military capabilities, communications and tactics.

Alexander received the privileged upbringing of a prince. He learnt to sing, hunt, ride, debate and read poetry. At the age of thirteen he was sent to a school run by the philosopher Aristotle that his father had established for young noblemen. Here Alexander was taught medicine, botany, zoology, politics and philosophy. He became 'a lover of learning and reading' and was so taken with the heroic tales of mythical soldiers such as Achilles – young, courageous men whose ambition and ability had no horizons – that he carried a copy of Homer's Iliad with him for the rest of his life. Moreover, the schoolfriends with whom he studied were to become his Companions – his closest associates on campaign, members of his élite cavalry.

Bust of Aristotle from the Louvre, Paris.

After three years with Aristotle, Alexander was brought back to the capital, Pella, and taught how to fight alongside his father. They made an incomparable team and the mighty Greek city-states such as Athens and Thebes, who had scorned their rural northern neighbours, soon answered to Macedonian rule.

In the summer of 336 BC, however, Philip was assassinated at his daughter's wedding. Alexander moved quickly and ruthlessly to secure the throne. The army offered its all-important support and Alexander became king. He was twenty years old.

The first task the new king faced was to secure the Macedonian hegemony that his father had imposed on the region. Alexander therefore swept rapidly through Greece, reinforcing control and making it clear that Philip's legacy was not to be rejected. Where necessary, he installed Macedonian garrisons or imposed leaders favourable to his cause. By the speed of his actions he held together the independent, often mutually hostile, Greek states in a federation under Macedonian control.

The states and kingdoms of the ancient world were largely divided by natural barriers. In an attempt to strengthen his borders, Alexander next went north, extending Macedonian rule to the River Danube. Resistance was fierce but Alexander displayed the determination and cunning that were to help him overcome many obstacles. At one stage he had to cross a mountain pass barricaded with wagons. He anticipated that the enemy would roll their wagons downhill at his troops, so he ordered them either to part ranks to let the wagons through or lie on the ground with their shields above them so that the wagons would ride over them. This successful tactic allowed Alexander's soldiers to charge the vulnerable enemy after they passed. Alexander's boldness, youthful energy and courage had overcome a complacent foe.

While Alexander was fighting in the north, the Greek city-state of Thebes, erroneously informed that he had been killed, declared its independence from the Greek Federation. To the Thebans' amazement, Alexander, who had just force-marched for thirteen days on hearing of this revolt, appeared outside their walls and, after a fierce assault, stormed the city. In revenge and as an example to all others, much of Thebes was destroyed and thousands of its inhabitants killed: 'every corner of the city was piled high with corpses'. Survivors were sold as slaves.

With the Greek states to his south and the Balkan lands in the north now secured, Alexander turned his attention to the next stage of his plan – the invasion and conquest of his powerful neighbour to the east – the Persian Empire.

By the time Alexander had taken over the reins of power, Macedonia was almost bankrupt. Although in financial difficulty himself, Alexander, before leaving for Persia, distributed expensive presents to those he was leaving behind in control. One colleague asked of him: 'But your majesty, what are you leaving for yourself?' to which Alexander replied: 'My hopes!'. Thus, aged twenty-one, with little more in the royal treasuries than 'hopes', Alexander set off at the head of his army, having declared war on the mightiest power in the world.

The Persian king, Darius III, was older than Alexander and considered competent and brave. His decision-making, however, was hampered by an assembly of courtiers who found it hard to agree on anything; certainly they were unsure how to deal with Alexander. Should they burn the land on his route? Or send their mighty navy to invade Greece in his absence? Initially, Darius hoped the force raised by his nobles in the west would, if not defeat Alexander, then at least scare him back to Macedonia. Alexander fought four major battles in his lifetime and the Battle of the River Granicus in 334 BC was the first. By their own standards, the Persian nobles had assembled a relatively small force of about 40,000 troops. The cavalry stood at the top of a steep river bank, with the infantry behind them. Alexander and his 35,000 men had arrived towards the end of the day. His experienced second-in-command Parmenio (who had been one of Philip's leading generals) advised his young king to wait until morning before attacking. Not for the last time, Alexander rebuked his subordinate for a lack of daring.

Alexander felt that an immediate attack would take the Persians by surprise. He had seen that the Persians had built some defences, an action Alexander interpreted as a sign of weakness: if an army had to build defences, it clearly did not believe in its own fighting abilities. Alexander decided that he would effect an even greater surprise by attacking the Persians' strongest position, their least expected point of assault. The attack was launched immediately and, though casualties were high, the Macedonians managed to cross the river and climb the muddy banks towards the

A Greek footsoldier fends off a Persian cavalryman, from a Red Figure Apulian vase. The armies of the vast Persian empire had excellent cavalry, but were at a disadvantage in the face of superior Macedonian infantry.

enemy. Before long the Macedonian cavalry and infantry were engaged in hand-to-hand fighting with the Persians: 'horse pressed against horse, man against man, wrestling with one another'.

Alexander, as always, led from the front and was an obvious target, easily recognizable by his shield and tall, white-plumed helmet. A javelin pierced his body-armour but failed to reach his flesh; a Persian brought his battle-axe crashing down upon Alexander's helmet, all but shearing it in two but, again, not even scratching the fortunate king. The same Persian was about to strike again when a Macedonian saw the danger and in one accurate blow cut off the opponent's arm at the shoulder. Having failed to kill Alexander, the Persians found themselves overwhelmed by the superior fighting force and fled. The battle was won and Persian casualties were high, particularly as Alexander executed all captured mercenaries.

Throughout his life Alexander gambled with his own mortality, preferring glory to longevity: 'It is a lovely thing to live with courage and to die leaving behind an everlasting renown.' Alexander was prepared to die, if it led to such greatness. Perhaps this absence of fear derived from the arrogance of a privileged youth, or the desire to exceed the achievements of his father. No doubt success also bred an inner confidence; from his earliest engagements until his death he never lost a battle. Alexander propagated this success. He exploited his victories and encouraged his soldiers to see in his fortune the guiding hands of the gods. Alexander believed that while 'God is the father of all mankind, it is the noblest and best whom he makes especially his own'. Soldiers prefer to fight believing that divine justice is on their side.

Although Alexander could have headed straight for Darius himself after the victory at Granicus, one of the great strengths of his strategy lay in always securing his communication and supply routes before advancing. As the Macedonian navy was weak, his inspired plan was to conquer the Persian navy's ports on the Mediterranean coast. With no bases it would be useless, and he would then not only have destroyed the enemy's sea power but also acquired it for himself. Only when he had taken control of the eastern Mediterranean did he move inland. Slowly, methodically and irresistibly, Alexander pushed forwards through his enemy's lands.

Darius began to prepare his response. He ordered his provinces to supply troops and, using some of the enormous wealth of the Persians, hired thousands of Greek mercenaries. Amongst these was the Greek naval leader, Memnon, who was assigned to take the still strong Persian fleet to Greece and Macedonia and stir up rebellion against Alexander. But when Memnon died of illness, Darius knew his future depended on the outcome of the next land battle. As he trusted neither the skill nor the luck of any of his generals, he decided he would lead the field himself. With an army of over 150,000 (estimates of its size vary enormously, some as high as 500,000, which would have been impossible to supply), Darius set out to destroy Alexander.

How did Alexander manage to defeat an army so much larger than his own? What was the key to his 'great' command? The answers lie in the exploitation of his army, his tactics, his use of psychology and his own example in battle. No commander can succeed unless the tools with which he is fighting are sufficient for the task, and Alexander had inherited from his father an army trained, equipped and motivated to the highest order. By the 5th century BC, Greek warfare had progressed significantly

A Greek phalanx, from the Chigi vase in the Museo di Villa Giulia, Rome. A phalanx consisted of hundreds of armoured infantrymen ranged side by side, advancing as a unified block against the enemy's formations.

since the man-to-man combat described by early authors such as Homer. Military service was still largely the province of those who could afford their own equipment but some city-states had introduced limited public funding for élite troops, while widespread poverty and unemployment ensured that there were thousands of potential mercenaries to be hired by anyone with the necessary finances.

Macedonian armies were organized around the phalanx – a large unit of infantry that stood normally sixteen men deep and hundreds wide. Each man carried a long defensive shield slung on his left arm and a pike held in both hands on his right side. When signalled by voice, trumpet or flute, these highly trained soldiers would advance against the opposing infantry in as unified a manner as they could manage. This was not a place for individual heroism, as the strength of a phalanx lay in the integrity of the group. The more cohesive they could remain, the less likely they were to be broken by the opposition.

It was considered a great honour to be in the army – life at this time offered few other privileges or means of raising one's status. The army was the state: the king, as head of state was thus the army's commander and from the moment the army approved the choice of the new monarch they gave him an absolute right of command over them. Only he enlisted men, decided on their leave, their punishments and their movements. The pay was meagre, but this was largely in order to encourage bravery in battle; wealth, in the form of booty, came only with victory.

Philip created a professional army, in which both noble cavalrymen and simple peasant infantry were trained to new standards. He imposed long training marches without the support of long baggage trains. He inflicted hours of drill practice and weapons training. He prohibited the traditional leave given soldiers in autumn so they could return home to deal with the harvest and he put an end to the common practice of halting operations in winter, due to the lack of food for men and forage for animals. He improved communications and supply, opened up promotions to talent rather than privilege, and developed better equipment. He organized the infantry into battalions (named after their commanding officer) that could operate both independently and as part of a coherent unit. As was traditional in the ancient world, the higher an officer's rank, the further to the right he was positioned in the battle-line. Philip's soldiers were given lighter shields and longer pikes (sarissas) which were up to 20 feet (7m) long. When manoeuvring, the points of the first five rows would protrude beyond the front lines preventing any breach of a coherently formed phalanx. At the same time he decided not to rely on these foot-soldiers (who were now to absorb the enemy attack or fix an enemy in place after charging them), expecting the mobile, offensive cavalry to deliver the knock-out blow.

Alexander had little reason to change the organization of his father's army. He sat at the core of the command structure, with a select group of cavalry noblemen called the 'Companions'. They acted as an advisory council and it was from this group that many governors of provinces were chosen. The arrangement of infantry in the centre with the cavalry on the wings remained unchanged. Tactically, everything was

Soldiers marching in formation, from the Nereid Monument of Xanthus in Lycia, 4th century BC.

geared towards this cavalry launching its pre-emptive killer blow, backed up by the brute, unified force of the phalanx which absorbed any enemy attack and could follow up on the cavalry's initial breakthrough. Working with both elements were hundreds of archers, javelin-throwers, lightly-armed soldiers, and shot-slingers.

Alexander's army numbered approximately 5,000 cavalry and 30,000 infantry, predominantly Macedonians, Greek allies and mercenaries. Alexander's army rarely exceeded 40,000: speed was crucial to his strategy and large numbers of troops would not have been able to move quickly along poor roads and through countryside that was much less populated and agriculturally developed than today. Even with this small force, Alexander sometimes split his army in two – an advance group followed up by the slower reserves and baggage wagons. To sustain this highly mobile army Alexander exploited the complex but efficient system of the Royal Roads that ran from the Aegean Sea to the heart of Persia. When necessary – especially in the east – Alexander also built new settlements and garrisons. He named up to a dozen of these new cities Alexandria, after himself. Later in his career, he set up a military training academy in Persia itself to provide replacement soldiers for those lost during campaigns.

Alexander was also accompanied by builders, engineers, architects, poets, an historian, a secretariat, scientists, physicians, servants and slave-traders. Although relatively lean and efficient, Alexander's army nevertheless resembled a small town crawling across the countryside. This travelling assembly was the effective hub, the administrative centre, of all that Alexander commanded. Wherever Alexander was, so too was the core of the expanding Macedonian empire.

Alexander always treated his soldiers well and they knew him to be a resourceful, courageous and good commander – one who would share the booty as and when it arose. But such considerations come at a cost, and Alexander knew that he had to quickly lead these men to success to maintain their loyalty. Thus he continually pushed himself to his physical limits: 'neither wine, nor sleep, nor sport, nor sex, nor spectacle, could ever distract his attention, as they did for other generals'. However, when occasion allowed, he could still enjoy the fruits of his position:

> He sat long over his wine because of his fondness for conversation. And although at other times his society was delightful and his manner full of charm beyond that of any prince of his age, yet when he was drinking he would sometimes become offensively arrogant. (*Plutarch*)

There were occasions when Alexander did not need his army to overcome obstacles. When campaigning through Persia in March 333 BC, and heading towards Darius, Alexander occupied the inland city of Gordium. This, the legendary city of King Midas, was known for its knot – a knot so elaborate and intricate that no one could untie it. The man who did was prophesied to become a great king. Alexander, unable to untangle it, drew his sword and slashed it in half, declaring the task accomplished. Such youthful audacity was just one of the reasons he was so greatly admired by his soldiers.

The Persian army was very different – it moved at only half the speed of the Macedonians. Plutarch explains that it was a 'tradition among the Persians not to begin a march until after sunrise'. Darius was too burdened with tradition and pomp, designed to impress and frighten those who gazed upon them. Once on the march the whole affair was almost embarrassingly cumbersome: carried at the head of the march were silver altars holding the sacred and eternal fire; then came ceremonial men and horses, then 'ten carts amply decorated with relief drawings in gold and silver'. These were followed by cavalry and infantry, all finely dressed, abundant with jewels; then the king himself on a gold and silver chariot, a magnificent display of wealth and ostentation. The king even brought with him his mother, wife, children, eunuchs and concubines.

> The Macedonians, on the other hand, provided a different spectacle: horses and men gleaming not with gold, not with multi-coloured clothes, but with iron and bronze. It was an army ready to stand its ground and follow its leader, and not overloaded with numbers and baggage . . . . Any location sufficed for their camp, any food for their provisions. (*Curtius*)

King Darius enthroned, attended by courtiers. Bas relief from the Palace of Xerxes at Persepolis.

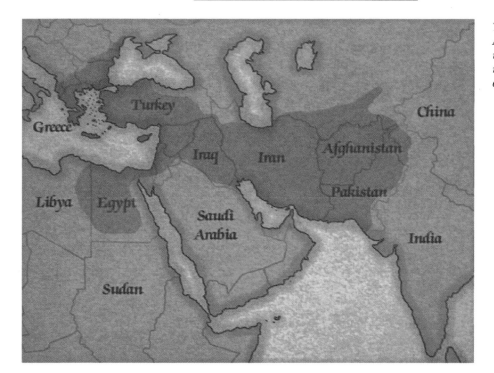

The full extent of Alexander's empire, with the outlines of the modern countries whose area it covered.

The world as perceived in the 4th century BC was but a fraction of its real size. Alexander, seeking Darius, had only the most rudimentary of maps to follow, aided by snippets of information he gathered from travellers and prisoners. Darius was unsure whether Alexander would attempt to pass through the Taurus Mountains, which would have provided a perfect eastern frontier to an expanded Macedonian empire. In fact, Alexander had already done so, breaching a key pass by sheer speed and surprise. Having crossed the mountains, he was now exploiting the fertile plains near the sea to feed and supply his troops.

Although neither king knew where they would eventually meet, both knew that location could be a decisive factor. Darius' advantage lay with the size of his army, so he needed a wide flat plain which would allow for the deployment and use of all his forces. Alexander preferred a narrower terrain in which tactics could prove decisive against a larger force, but, full of self-belief, he was confident he would win wherever he fought.

The Persians encamped on a wide plain near modern Antakya and waited for Alexander, but, near Adana, Alexander fell sick. Darius grew impatient: he had a large army to feed and could not sustain delay. He wondered whether Alexander was scared or had changed direction. Whatever the reason, Darius decided he would decamp and attempt to find his enemy.

The two armies approached each other near the north-eastern corner of the Mediterranean. A narrow range of mountains runs along the coast and Alexander was on the western side travelling south, while Darius was on the eastern side heading north. Both were unaware of the other's movements. Darius then chose a pass that Alexander had left unguarded and crossed, unopposed, down to the coast. There he heard, to his surprise, that Alexander was now to his south, so he turned to follow him. Alexander was now being approached from the rear, his lines of retreat and supply cut off.

Darius arrived at Issus, where he encountered a camp of Alexander's sick and wounded soldiers. These he mutilated by cutting off their hands to prevent them fighting again. He then advanced a little further south until he reached the small River Pinarus that ran the two miles (3km) from the mountains on Darius' left down to the sea on his right. Here he stopped and established a defensive position on the north bank. Historians have criticized Darius for stopping but, in fact, it was a perfectly intelligent response. He had been repeatedly told that Alexander's strength lay in his phalanx, so what better to break the cohesion on which it relied than a river with difficult banks? Darius knew the tactic had not succeeded at Granicus but this time he was in charge and he hoped for greater success. The cohesive mass of Alexander's phalanx, with its long pikes, would certainly otherwise be unbreakable by the Persian phalanx who were still using much shorter, overhead spears. There was another reason Darius did not wish to go any further south: only a few miles away, the mountains curved into the sea and his army would easily be trapped in such a spot. Anyway, Darius saw no need to chase Alexander further – he was certain that Alexander would turn and attack him.

One reason Alexander had returned to the coast after Gordium was to liaise with his fleet, which he always maintained to shadow and supply his land campaigns. When he received the astonishing report that Darius was behind him, Alexander immediately sent one of his ships up the coast to investigate. To his amazement the galley confirmed the report. One of the characteristics of great command is the ability to accept surprising new information and respond immediately without disorder or panic. Alexander did just this; his quick, decisive mind summed up the changed situation and he turned the army around.

After a brief night's rest, he marched the army from before dawn until just after midday until they finally saw Darius's troops stretched across the horizon. This was the point at which Alexander's tactical abilities came to the fore. He looked across at the lines of troops before him and considered his response. His first action, as the plain widened before him, was to bring his cavalry up from the rear and assign them to either side of the advancing infantry. The nearer they got to the river, the wider the plain became. Alexander could see that Darius had positioned his infantry along the river while deploying a force of approximately 10,000 cavalry by the sea. There seemed to be very little cavalry between the infantry and the mountains. Other troops, obviously intending to come behind Alexander during the battle, could be seen in the wooded hills.

In response, Alexander sent Parmenio with most of the 5,000 cavalry to the left wing and told him to stay close to the sea, so that the Persians could not get behind him. Although they were greatly outnumbered, Alexander spread out his infantry, by

A Greek Trireme, a sea-going ship with three banks of oars, circa 400BC. Warships were powered by oarsmen rather than sails, which restricted them to coastal waters and left them dependent on their shore base.

reducing the depth of his lines, to match the length of Darius' front. In this way, he effectively reduced Darius' numerical advantage; in a fighting zone restricted to the two miles (3km) between sea and mountains, many tens of thousands of Darius' troops remained behind the lines and could play no part.

Alongside the infantrymen and cavalry, both sides also deployed their slingers, archers and javelin-throwers. Darius had many such troops but while they were effective on broken, steep or wooded ground where it was difficult for the cavalry or infantry to bear down upon them, on flat land they were vulnerable and of less value.

Darius himself then took up the customary Persian royal position in the centre, somewhat behind the front lines and surrounded by bodyguards, and watched as Alexander continued his slow, careful advance in his direction. Despite the dust and confusion of troop movements, the two commanders were clearly visible to their own soldiers: Alexander on horseback and Darius on his ceremonial chariot. By the end of the day, one of these great leaders would be defeated, his army destroyed.

Having made his major deployments, Alexander now considered final alterations. Whereas Darius misunderstood or misjudged Alexander's strengths, Alexander immediately understood Darius' tactics. First, hiding them behind the dust raised by infantry movements, he re-deployed his cavalry including some of his own élite horsemen to reinforce Parmenio's defence. Then he sent a small force to clear away Darius' minor deployment in the foothills. Alexander's plan was for Parmenio to hold Darius' main attack while he crashed through the Persian infantry deployed by the hills. The phalanx, meanwhile, would attempt to cross the river to engage and, at very least, parry the Persians. If the Macedonian phalanx was the hardened belly of the army, the cavalry were its fists: Alexander, who would lead the 300 best horse-men on the right, intended to launch the knock-out blow. He realized he had one chance – to strike at the heart of the Persian army and Darius himself. He was sure that if he could kill or capture their king, then the enemy army would collapse.

The armies of Alexander and Darius prepare to engage across the river Pinarus at the Battle of Issus.

Alexander's psychological preparations were vital. He may have been outnumbered but his own troops were much better prepared than the Persians for the conflict that lay ahead of them. He motivated them and made them 'hungry for battle'. This was his great skill – the ability to inspire his men so that they would, if necessary, die for him. Without that loyalty, a commander such as Alexander would have achieved little.

How did he inspire them so well? Largely, by his unfailing willingness to fight alongside them as both friend and comrade ' . . . he exercised with his men, he made his appearance and dress little different from an ordinary citizen's, he had the energy of a soldier' (*Curtius*). After the battles, often injured himself, the first action of a weary Alexander was always to visit the wounded and offer words of encouragement. Alexander's lack (or suppression) of fear was perhaps his greatest attribute. This allowed him to lead his troops wherever he wanted them to go. Once a battle started his troops knew that their commander was at the front risking his life and that their duty was to follow and fight to protect him.

His management of the army was logistically practical and psychologically astute. His men were well-fed and promptly paid. He would see them when he could and listen to their grievances. He drank with some, and saw them entertained and well-rested. The brave received decoration, the sick received care. At the same time, when necessary, he would ruthlessly bribe, punish or kill. Some of his soldiers would shake at the memory of Alexander for years after his death. Superhuman though he may have appeared, he never forgot that his soldiers were ordinary humans susceptible to homesickness, fear, loneliness, sexual frustration, boredom and bad weather. This outward appearance of love and concern, allied with his courage and determination, evoked great affection from his soldiers. 'These characteristics, whether they were natural or consciously cultivated had made him in the eyes of his men as much an object of affection as of awe.' (*Curtius*)

Now, as battle loomed, Alexander brought these soldiers slowly towards their Persian adversaries. They were eager to attack but Alexander kept the advance deliberate and controlled: he wanted to make sure that the Persians saw exactly what was coming at them. The Persians, who had felt relatively confident in the sheer size of their force, began to have second thoughts. Their morale began to waver, and the failure of Darius and his officers to correct the situation meant that the slightest misfortune to befall them could cause disaster.

Alexander, however, rode along his front line offering words of encouragement to stir up troops. He also addressed individuals and particular groups, telling the Macedonians that they were liberators of the world, reminding the Greeks that the Persians deserved punishment for their past invasions of Greece, inciting the allies and mercenaries to look at the enemy line gleaming in gold and purple and think of the booty ready for the taking. Individual commanders were then told to pass these words of encouragement back down the lines.

Then, without warning, the battle began: Alexander charged across the river and hit the archers opposite him. The very appearance of the Macedonians, yelling and splashing through the water, terrorized the men along the opposite bank and they fled.

Alexander and Darius confront each other at the Battle of Issus, from a Roman mosaic found at Pompeii, in the Museo Nazionale di Napoli.

The Persian infantry and small amount of cavalry behind the archers also collapsed in the face of Alexander and his onslaught, and the Macedonians swept through them, sparing no one. Meanwhile, Alexander's phalanx had broken, as Darius had hoped, due to the speed with which Alexander had moved and the obstruction of the river banks. Some Macedonians had reached the other side while others were still struggling to cross the river. The fighting was bitter and casualties on both sides were high:

> ... the blood really flowed, for the two lines were so closely interlocked that they were striking each other's weapons with their own and driving their blades into their opponent's faces ... only by bringing down his opponent could each man advance. (*Curtius*)

In the centre, some of the Persian-employed Greek mercenaries gained the upper hand and began to exact a heavy toll on the Macedonians. Alexander now wheeled his cavalry towards Darius' centre. Darius watched with alarm as his left wing collapsed in the face of Alexander's approach. His personal bodyguard fought bravely but Darius realized – or believed – that nothing would stop Alexander from reaching him. Preferring to survive the battle and fight again, he turned and fled.

Darius' flight was in some ways premature, for the battle had not been entirely lost. By the sea, the Persians were slowly gaining the upper hand and threatening to encircle the Macedonians; the relatively thin lines of Alexander's infantry were beginning to tear apart. But when they realized that their own commander had abandoned them, the Persians lost all heart and turned to flee.

A retreating army is easy prey and, in the mêlée, many were trampled underfoot or, because of their armour, soon caught by lightly-armoured Macedonian troops in bloody pursuit. Alexander and his father Philip were innovators in the vigorous pursuit of a defeated foe and no pity was shown; it was accepted that the more that were killed now, the more enduring the victory. Tens of thousands of Darius' finest soldiers were killed and even though Darius lived to fight again, he would never again have at his disposal the high quality front-line troops that he had at Issus. Alexander's policy of annihilation, cruel though it was, paid dividends. Persian casualties were huge – perhaps as high as 100,000. The Macedonians, by contrast, had lost only a few hundred.

The battle was Alexander's. Despite being surprised by Darius' strategic moves, Alexander had displayed quickness of mind by turning his army around and arriving at the battleground before the enemy had fully prepared his defences or tactical preparations. Once there, Alexander had watched as Darius deployed and then matched his lines from the sea to the hills and had made two important tactical adjustments – more cavalry to the seaward side and sufficient troops to the hills to parry any attempt to get behind his lines. Then he had brought his troops forward slowly and in good order. He had fired them with courage, greed and revenge and, at a given moment, unleashed his attack. Leading by example, he had brought his élite cavalry upon the weaker hillward flank of Darius' army and delivered such a blow that, in a short time, the king – the linch-pin of the Persian army – had turned and fled. It had been a great risk: had Alexander been killed or had his attack stalled, then Darius' men would almost certainly have swamped and defeated the Macedonian invaders.

The battle ended at sunset when lack of light prevented further pursuit. Alexander's dead were cremated, the wounded were helped, the Persian camp looted and the prisoners dealt with. Although Alexander had been wounded in the thigh, one of his first acts was, as always, to visit the rudimentary field hospital to console and congratulate his wounded compatriots. There he chatted to his valiant troops, asked them how their injuries had been received, and, 'allowed them to exaggerate as much as they liked'.

If the Battle of Issus demonstrated Alexander's tactical prowess, its aftermath showed his political astuteness. Among the prisoners were Darius' wife, mother and two children. Distraught, they feared rape and death, but Alexander informed them they would be treated as royalty and he vowed they would remain untouched by him or any other man. This chivalry towards defeated royalty (though not its army) was characteristic of Alexander and became part of a romantic image that has lasted through the centuries. So well did he treat Darius' mother that she committed suicide when he died. His treatment of these prisoners was just the first in a series of conciliatory actions which won him respect and, crucially, allegiance from those he had defeated. Alexander saw the political advantages of unity between diverse peoples. He was an adept politician, skilled in the arts of intrigue and manipulation, fluent in the languages of both the victors and the vanquished.

His primary concern was always his lines of communication and supply. Though he and his army lived largely off the lands through which they passed, the links with his rear were vital. Troop replacements, mail, extra supplies – all had to be brought along secure routes. If Alexander could ally himself with the peoples through whose lands he passed, he greatly increased his chances of protecting these lines. How could he maintain control of these native populations? The solution was not to dominate and rule by fear – it would not have been possible – but to share power with them. Is it not better, Alexander asked them, to acknowledge me as king and thus keep your provinces than to remain loyal to a weak king like Darius? He also won over the religious hierarchies in Egypt and Babylonia. Alexander was never too proud to bow before the gods of other nations; to do otherwise could have been fatal.

To limit the inherent dangers, the pragmatic Alexander did, however, make sure he placed military control in Macedonian hands. He also took time to persuade his own troops not to destroy the lands they passed through or alienate the peoples they had defeated.

Darius, once safely on the other side of the Euphrates River, sent a message to Alexander offering a peace treaty (partly because he wanted his family back) which offered Alexander control of all the land to the west of the Euphrates – that is, all of Asia Minor, Syria, Phoenicia and Egypt – as well as large sums of money and Darius' daughter in marriage. Parmenio told Alexander that if he were Alexander he would

The presumed site of the Battle of Issus, near the town of Iskenderun in South East Turkey named after Alexander the Great.

accept. Alexander replied that if he were Parmenio so would he, but he was Alexander and he would not. Alexander sent his reply to Darius: all the Persian king's land, money and even daughters were already his and if Darius wanted them back he would have to fight for them.

The Persian king had escaped this time but both sides knew he was beaten. Alexander could have chased him but knew there were more important tasks to be undertaken first. Before heading into the centre of Persia, he needed to be sure that his lines of communication with Macedonia and Greece were absolutely safe. To do this meant finally crushing the Persian fleet by capturing their remaining Mediterranean ports in Lebanon and Phoenicia.

One of these was at Tyre which believed itself to be utterly safe within its defences and scorned Alexander's claims that they were soon to fall before him. They offered Alexander a non-belligerence agreement but he refused and laid siege. The old city had been abandoned and all the inhabitants had moved to the 'new' city on an island almost half-a-mile (1km) from the shore. Behind its high walls they resented, but did not fear, the Macedonian threat.

Alexander, however, had his answer: he blockaded the city with ships and then began to build a wide causeway from the shore, with the intention of reaching the island. Locals were forced to carry rock and stone and good progress was made. Over a matter of weeks the causeway got closer and closer until the Tyrians began to have second thoughts – indeed, they shipped their women and children to north

Africa. Soon, both sides were within artillery range and the Tyrians began catapulting rocks upon the workers on the causeway. Alexander was able to respond with his own technology – he built two 150-foot (46m) towers, covered in animal skins to deflect fire-balls, on which he put two large catapults that could propel heavy stone balls hundreds of feet. The Tyrians responded by sending fire-ships and setting the towers ablaze. Alexander then widened the causeway (which still exists) and rebuilt the towers. Meanwhile he sent ships alongside the fortress. The Tyrians countered by dropping hot sand on the crews, who were badly burnt when the sand fell between their protective armour and skin. The Tyrians then dropped rocks until the waters were too shallow for ships. Alexander resorted to dredging, but the Tyrians used divers to cut the cables of the transport ships.

So it went on until at last Alexander managed to ram through the walls using logs mounted on ships and was able to storm the city. The seige, which had lasted seven months, was over and the Macedonians, again displaying a post-battle orgiastic glory in revenge, released their pent-up frustration by engaging in appalling slaughter. Despite the fact that 7,000 Tyrians had already died in Tyre's defence, 2,000 more were now crucified. The remaining 30,000 were sold into slavery.

Ports such as Gaza suffered the same fate, and within months Alexander commanded the Mediterranean east of Greece by virtue of the fact that he controlled its major ports. The Persian fleet collapsed, as expected, and was never again to pose any threat. Alexander then occupied northern Egypt. Of all the cities that Alexander created in his name, it was here in Egypt that the most famous and enduring was founded: Alexandria. Homer, Alexander's favourite poet, is said to have inspired the choice of site and, legend tells us, Alexander himself marked out the location of the new city's walls with a trail of barley.

Only now did Alexander head eastward towards the heart of the Persian empire and his third major battle. Darius had amassed another huge army, but although the psychological effect on Alexander's troops may well have been great, Alexander himself knew that he faced many raw, uninspired recruits. Much of the cream of Persian soldiery and finest Greek mercenaries had perished at Issus. The battle that followed, at Gaugamela, nevertheless required very skilful command to secure victory. Darius tried to encircle the Macedonians but Alexander prevented this move and increasingly stretched the Persian lines by an oblique advance until he could launch a counter-attack against them. Meanwhile, Darius had sent up to 300 chariots toward the Macedonians but this too failed, for Alexander had prepared his lines to open and let them through, then close and leave them to be dealt with by his rear-line troops. Once again, Darius was forced to flee. He would pose no further threat, and shortly after was assassinated by his own officers.

Alexander now marched on to the great Persian cities of Babylon and Susa (both rich beyond expectation in precious metals, cloth and craftworks), and then took the ceremonial centre of Persia – Persepolis. He had to fight his way through a number of mountain passes to get there but the reward was worth it: there was so much treasure

Entrance to the Palace of Darius at Persepolis.

Head of Alexander the Great, from Pergamon, 2nd century BC, in the Istanbul Archaelogical Museum.

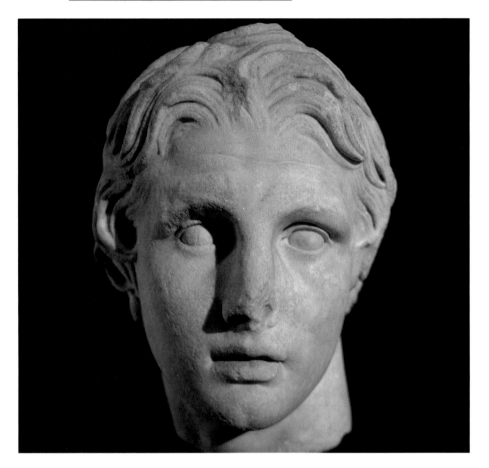

that it took 'two thousand pairs of mules and five hundred camels' to carry it all away. In celebrating the end of war between himself and the Persians, Alexander and his companions burnt down the palace at Persepolis – an act of vandalism regretted by Alexander the next morning and by archaeologists ever since.

Alexander now faced the problem of securing his position throughout Persia. He had extracted a military victory but he knew that if his empire was to endure he had to win the allegiance of the Persian people. To this end, he continued to offer them partnership and participation. Within his own court he introduced Persian etiquette (partly no doubt, because he preferred the sensual charms of Persia to the harsher manners of Macedonia). He appointed Persian governors and was careful to ingratiate himself with the nobility. Alexander's policy of reconciliation and friendship, first seen in his treatment of Darius' family at Issus, displayed his genius at winning over a defeated enemy.

He continued east, entering land that neither he nor his men had seen before – where natural obstacles and fear of the unknown were enemies as great as the people they fought. The weather was, at times, so inhospitable as to jeopardize the entire venture. To make matters worse, those he now fought adopted a sensible policy of small-scale skirmishing and ambush – a tactic that which was, and remains, much more difficult to deal with. Before he could travel to the edges of the 'Ocean' (the mythical waters that encircled the world) he still had to secure the many peripheral provinces of his new empire. Alexander was one of the few great commanders able to deal effectively with partisan warfare. His victory over the Scythians at Jaxartes in particular, was the only time in pre-Roman warfare that these tribes were bettered. Alexander was frequently wounded – a splintered shin-bone, concussion, arrow wounds – but his motivation never paled. There was only one direction that interested him – and that was forward. Aristotle had taught him that the world extended from Spain in the west to India in the east. Alexander intended to conquer all of it.

However, constant hard fighting against an elusive enemy and the prospect of perpetual advance began to sap the enthusiasm of his troops. Discontent first manifested itself among the officer class at court who had direct experience of Alexander's increasing penchant for oriental practices: they resented the way in which they, the victors, were now being asked to share equal standing with those they had defeated. When Alexander suggested the court follow the Persian tradition of prostration before its leader, more pockets of rebellion sprang up. For these gruff veterans, the young king had gone too far. To the Greek and Macedonian mind prostration was only offered to the gods. Their king, while a great man and seemingly invincible, was not their god. Nevertheless, Alexander did not stray from his policy of conciliation. He knew that he could not conquer all of Persia, or the lands further east, if he did not offer brotherhood to the Persians and a part in his army to their troops. Alexander found himself facing major internal dissension, prompting him to show his brutal, tyrannical side: he executed a number of men including the trusty old general Parmenio on suspicion of plotting against him.

Achilles fighting Memnon, from a 4th century BC Attic vase. Although his family claimed descent from the hero Herakles, Alexander identified most strongly with Achilles, hero of Homer's accounts of the Trojan wars. He is said to have regretted not having an historian of the stature of Homer to record his own exploits.

In 327 BC, as a further sign of his desire for assimilation between the two cultures, he married a Persian, Roxane. Although a marriage of some political gain – Roxane's father brought with him peace in a northern province – Alexander clearly saw it as a symbolic gesture of unification between east and west. Curtius wrote that Alexander considered it important that 'Persians and Macedonians be joined in wedlock; that only in that way could shame be taken from the conquered and haughtiness from the victors.'

Having finally silenced the opposition in the north – not without supreme effort and sacrifice – Alexander proceeded to India. Although the army's enthusiasms were further dampened by the continued fierceness of the natives they fought, they nevertheless battled their way through the Hindu Kush, past Kabul and into north-west India. One battle led to the capture of up to a quarter of a million cattle, the best of which Alexander sent back to Macedonia to improve the breeding stock. Such successes were, however, increasingly hard to come by, and the men continued to grow weary.

Many Indian leaders, aware in advance of Alexander's notoriety, surrendered without a fight. One, King Porus, however, did not and Alexander fought his fourth, and final, major engagement. Porus ranged his army on the east bank of the River Hydaspes in anticipation of Alexander's arrival. The river, half a mile (1km) wide and

Frieze from the Alexander Sarcophagus found at Sidon. Abdalonymus, for whom the sarcophagus was probably made, was a Phoenician whom Alexander installed as King of Sidon.

fast flowing, was virtually impassable and Porus was defending any possible fords. An opposed river crossing is a complicated and difficult operation and Alexander's success in doing so was masterful. He began by keeping Porus and his men awake by noisy night-time feints and deployments. Gradually the enemy's resilience and alertness were worn down. One night, under the cover of a storm, Alexander took most of his army about twenty miles (32km) upstream and made a treacherous crossing using inflated animal skins as floats. Porus was taken by surprise, though by the time Alexander had marched upon him, he had managed to prepare his 200 elephants and many thousands of troops to do battle. The key was to avoid sending the cavalry against the elephants because the horses would have shied off. Instead, Alexander sent infantry to attack the Indian flanks, causing a panic which sent troops running into the centre for cover. This prompted the elephants to move. First, they approached and trampled the Macedonian phalanx but, attacked and slashed (elephants have thin skins) by lightly armoured troops, they turned and stampeded their own men. Unable to control the massive animals, the Indians soon fell into disorder and the battle was lost. Porus brought himself before Alexander and offered his surrender. 'How do you wish to be treated?' asked Alexander. 'As a king,' replied Porus. This was the kind of response that Alexander appreciated and he allowed Porus to continue as monarch.

A soldier binds the wounds of his companion.

Not long after the defeat of Porus, Alexander's army finally could take no more and mutinied. They had been on the march for eight years and had journeyed fifteen, perhaps twenty thousand miles (25000–32000km). The weather was bad – none had heard of or experienced a monsoon before – the land was strange, they were ill and homesick. They had earned their reward and wanted to spend it. They did not want to die fighting in yet another foreign land. They saw no advantage in continuing and were uninterested in Alexander's wish to reach the 'Ocean'. Although he tried to change their minds, this time Alexander had no choice but to turn back.

For Alexander this must have been a great disappointment for he was still trying to emulate and exceed the deeds of the legendary gods and heroes. Like Achilles in the *Iliad*, Alexander made it clear that he would prefer a short life but one that would live in the memories of men for ever, rather than a longer, more anonymous existence. Life after death at this time was seen as a shadowy, inconsequential state unless you had, in life, become deified and entered the pantheon of the gods. This could only be achieved through success. Alexander constantly thirsted after such glories to prove to all that he was worthy of such an elevated position. He did not seem to realize that he had already secured his place in history.

Even as the army turned back the fighting continued. Alexander refused to travel the way he had come, instead insisting on travelling south down the River Indus to find its mouth and see if trade could be initiated between it and the River Euphrates. Thereafter, he and his army made an arduous, decimating journey back to Babylon. Alexander himself was almost killed by a lung wound in one fight and, while travelling through the Gedrosian Desert, many of his troops and most non-combatants and animals died of thirst and starvation.

Despite all these difficulties, he continued to work towards assimilation of the western and eastern elements of his huge empire. He made Babylon the capital and presided over the simultaneous marriage of a large group of his officers to Persian women. He too married again – the daughter of his old adversary, Darius. Despite this his grip on the veteran Macedonians remained strong: when he attempted to pension off some soldiers in 324 BC and send them home, the old soldiers mutinied at what they interpreted as a disgrace – they wanted to stay with Alexander.

Alexander the Great. Detail from the Issus Mosaic in the Museo Nazionale di Napoli.

He continued to plan new campaigns – Arabia and northern Africa. But, after so many wounds and so much hardship, his body was unable to fight off what appears to have been a fever and he died in June, 323 BC. He was thirty-two years old.

Alexander lived and fought primarily for himself, rather than the glory of Macedonia, and had given little thought to his succession: he had, after all, expected to reign for some years to come and had been wary of producing sons who could grow up to be rivals while he was still campaigning. When asked, on his death bed, to whom he left his empire, he replied 'to the strongest'. His empire collapsed into rivalry, intrigue and disarray. For decades, there was a desperate struggle between leading members of his army to secure control but none emerged as a credible successor. Even Alexander's wives and son were killed in the bloody, unresolved struggle.

What exactly is it that defines Alexander as a great commander? Countless battles have been fought and won through the ages but why does Alexander's name rank above the many and good captains and officers over the centuries?

It is in part because he was a genius of grand strategy. Building colonies and protecting his lines of communication are but one element of this. He moved systematically towards declared objectives, never rushing from one location to the next without considering the implications. He preferred to allow Darius time to build up his army while he neutralized the Persian fleet by capturing their land bases around the Mediterranean. He had no over-arching doctrine: he dealt with every city, district or province as best suited his needs. Alexander was not trying to improve the world, he was trying to explore and control it. An important part of his strategy was propaganda, at which he excelled – not least in being probably the first to specifically choose to take chroniclers and historians on campaign with him.

War was a bloody business. Cities that resisted him were, once conquered, subjected to appalling retribution. Potential soldiers were killed and women and children sold into slavery. Thebes, Tyre, Gaza, all suffered such a fate. The great palace of Persepolis was maliciously burned to the ground. Alexander was a court intriguer who never loosened his grip. Cleitus – who had saved Alexander's life at Granicus – was killed in a drunken rage; plotters, including his own historian Callisthenes, were killed; and even Parmenio, the senior general who fought with Alexander through most of the Persian campaign, was assassinated. These bloody, sometimes callous, acts were those of a man determined, irrespective of all else, to maintain total, unchallenged control. There was certainly much brutality in Alexander's world but perhaps no commander in his, or any other period, achieves greatness without a streak of such ruthlessness.

Alexander changed the course of world history because he was as much a great conqueror as a great commander. The previous barriers between west and east were weakened and, in the next generation, Greek-speaking settlers flooded east. Commercial links developed between the western Mediterranean and the Indian subcontinent, and soon beyond that to the far east. Alexandria, in Egypt, became the leading port of the Mediterranean and a crossroads of international trade. Indirectly he had prepared the way for the introduction and spread of both Christianity and Islam across Europe and Asia. Above all, he introduced the image of the all-conquering, heroic leader that has influenced the military mind, for better or worse, ever since.

The extent of his conquests lies at the heart of subsequent adulation. Commanders such as Caesar and Napoleon looked to Alexander and were in awe of the young man's ambition and achievements. Many have tried to emulate him, but Alexander was the first great commander and therefore in many ways the most impressive. Those who followed – like Caesar – found the task much more daunting because, after Alexander, the standards by which they would be judged by history had risen to new heights.

CHAPTER TWO

JULIUS CAESAR

'He . . . shrank from no speech or action . . .
to get possession of the objects for which he strove.' (Dio)

Unlike Alexander, Gaius Julius Caesar was first and foremost a politician. For him, military command was the most appropriate way of seizing control of Rome rather than conquering the known world. As a commander, he made mistakes and faced defeat on a number of occasions. He had little military training and relied heavily on his soldiers. He often broke the laws and requirements of the state for which he was fighting. Yet, despite this, Caesar's abilities and achievements as a commander have secured his name in military history.

Caesar is the prime example of the skilled politician as commander. He was a brilliant orator, showed a complete understanding of man-management and was ruthless and manipulative. He was willing to lead from the front when necessary but preferred to organize rather than fight. Even his errors served only to educate him and illustrate his considerable talent at turning bad fortune, as much as good, to his advantage.

Caesar is said to have been tall, fair, and well-built . . . . His health was sound . . . but he twice had epileptic fits while on campaign . . . . His baldness was a disfigurement which his enemies harped upon, much to his exasperation; and he used to comb the thin strands of hair forward.' (*Suetonious*).

Rome was founded in about 750 BC, and for hundreds of years was ruled by kings. These increasingly unpopular monarchs were eventually replaced by a republic. By the time Caesar was born, around 100 BC, this republic had spread its control throughout Italy and most of the Mediterranean basin, including large parts of Spain and northern Africa. Rome's conquests had brought it great rewards, but the economy had become dependent on the fruits of expansion. The rich amassed

Statue of Julius Caesar.

Roman senators depicted on a frieze from the Ara Pacis Augustae, Rome.

wealth by using cheap slave labour, while Roman workers became unemployed. Caesar thus grew up in a period of unrest and civil war, and as a member of one of Rome's oldest aristocratic families was well placed to view the corruption and discord that increasingly pervaded Roman society. To Caesar it was very clear how the political administration operated: money was the key that unlocked the doors to power.

It was always expected of the young Julius that, on completing his education, he would assume a modest place on the long ladder of administrative and political office. However, his father, Lucius, died when Caesar was only fifteen and, free of patriarchal authority, he quickly discarded any remaining family expectations that he would accept a life of middle-ranking civil service. His first move was to break off an existing engagement and instead marry into a more significant family.

> He showed himself perfectly ready to serve and flatter everybody, even ordinary persons . . . he did not mind temporarily grovelling. (*Dio*)

Caesar's early aspirations, as well as some family connections with out-of-favour political figures, did not go unnoticed by the current regime and he was arrested. Influential friends had him released, but it seemed prudent for the nineteen-year-old to leave Rome and enter temporary military service. His first posting was in the Near East, as aide-de-camp to a provincial governor, after which he went to Cilicia, one of Alexander the Great's old stomping-grounds. During this period, he proved himself a brave and courageous young soldier and won acclaim for saving the life of a comrade.

After serving, it is believed, in the armies that crushed Spartacus' slave rebellion, Caesar left the army but still considered it unwise to return to Rome. He spent some time in the south as a student of Rhetoric. The skills he learnt were to prove invaluable – the ability to articulate, cajole and persuade are crucial to any leader, whether military or civil, and Caesar would later exploit them to the full.

> Do you know any man who, even if he has concentrated on the art of oratory to the exclusion of all else, can speak better than Caesar? (*Cicero*)

The political atmosphere in Rome remained unsafe and Caesar decided to winter on the island of Rhodes. En route his ship was captured by pirates, who kept him prisoner for nearly forty days, until a large ransom could be paid. During his captivity he joked with his captors that, once released, he would seek them out, capture and crucify them. They laughed at his arrogance – but after his release, that was exactly what he did.

Finally, after having organized a force to defend Roman property on the coast of Asia Minor (modern Turkey), he felt confident enough to return home. The regime had changed and Caesar's deeds were recognized. As reward, he was elected to an administrative post in the highly structured political hierarchy. Each stage was clearly marked, most notably with age restrictions, and Caesar could now work towards becoming a senator, or better still, a consul – one of the two senators annually elected to rule Rome.

Throughout his twenties, Caesar strove constantly to improve his status. His attack was two-pronged. On the one hand he spoke on behalf of popular themes and projects, gaining both political and public support. At the same time, he sought alliances with the 'right' people, borrowing extensively in order to lavish gifts and bribes upon anyone who could be of the slightest use. Although this was standard senatorial practice, Caesar stood out as the most extravagant buyer of favours.

After a year on an official posting in Spain – where, in Cadiz, he wept before a statue of Alexander the Great, on realizing that by the time Alexander had reached Caesar's age he had conquered most of the known world – Caesar returned to Rome more determined than ever to fulfil his political ambitions. Caesar would involve himself with anyone who could further his career. His relationships, both in and out of wedlock, became notorious. His first wife had died and Caesar, now aged thirty-two, remarried, once more into a politically useful family. He divorced his second wife soon afterwards, however, on suspicion of adultery (the adultery was unproven but Caesar piously declared that he could not live with a woman even suspected of such an act as it would darken his name). Any scandal – real or imagined – could be used against him, and he could not risk that: rivals were always waiting for a chance to ruin him. For the next few years he continued to ingratiate himself with fellow senators and the general populace with bribes, huge public shows, gladiatorial contests, athletic games and banquets. Plutarch recounts that: 'He gained so much upon the people, that everyone was eager to find out new offices and new honours for him in return for his munificence.'

Caesar knew that his popularity with the public was standing him in good stead but all this was costing an enormous amount of money – and his creditors were calling in the debts. He tried to get control of Egypt but this was refused him by the Senate: many senators increasingly disliked the way this brash young man was building up a strong, independent client-system of his own. Caesar, undaunted, bribed his way to the post of Chief Priest (Pontifex Maximus) – a religious posting that made his person sacrosanct in the eyes of the law, thus preventing at least some of his opponents from taking action against him.

Rome's armies were usually commanded by senior politicians, often ex-consuls, who represented both the Roman people and the Senate – the 'senatus populusque Romanus' (SPQR). Political and military command went hand-in-hand and the beauty of the Roman army was that it could still win battles even in the hands of the weakest political appointee. But there were clearly disadvantages to this system: military objectives would change from commander to commander, political requirements could overshadow military experience, and conquest was as much for personal gain as for the benefit of the Roman state. Armies became instruments of individual political ambition, as Caesar clearly knew and later exemplified. In 60 BC, Caesar, aged forty-one, was awarded a one-year provincial governorship of Further Spain. Trouble had been brewing between local tribes and their Roman rulers, and Caesar exploited

Interior of the Senate.

The restored Senate building in Rome, extended and much altered after Caesar's death.

this to the full, gaining both military experience and earning himself some valuable booty. He learnt that war could be both politically and financially profitable.

Back in Rome, in 59 BC, Caesar formed a valuable pact with two very powerful allies – Pompey, Rome's most successful commander, and Crassus, Rome's wealthiest man. The pact helped Caesar finally to achieve his ambition of being elected consul. This group – with Caesar as its consular representative – was so powerful that the co-consul Bibulus was effectively ousted and spent most of the year at home complaining.

Caesar was thus enabled to govern alone and do very much as he pleased. It became a joke to sign and seal bogus documents not: '. . . during the Consulship of Bibulus and Caesar' but instead 'during the Consulship of Julius and Caesar'. (*Suetonious*)

Once in office, Caesar devoted a good deal of effort to public needs: cancelling tax demands on farmers; dividing public land among fathers of three or more children; and so on. This was done partly out of genuine concern and partly for political expediency. He also remarried, again to a daughter of another influential family, while his own daughter was married off to Pompey to cement that alliance.

As his twelve-month consulship neared its end, Caesar had to think quickly what his next move should be. Ex-consuls were automatically given postings as governors, and as governor he would be above the law and free from having to answer any charges against him. Some of the Senate, worried about what he would do with a provincial army, tried to appoint him to a non-military area. They were unsuccessful: Caesar had too many powerful friends. Although rumour had it that during his consulship he replaced gold ingots in the treasury with gold-plated bronze bars, he was still being hounded for debt and wanted a potentially rich source of plunder. Eventually he

*Ruins of the Forum,
centre of public life in
Rome.*

secured three provinces on Italy's northern borders: Cisalpine Gaul, Illyricum and (by great fortune – due to the sudden, presumably accidental death of its governor) Transalpine Gaul.

Governors were also the military commanders of their provinces and expected to campaign at the head of their armies. Caesar was only too happy to do so as he had immediately decided that he would expand Roman conquests as far as he could: the more gold he could amass, the more people in Rome he could coerce.

The Roman army has assumed a semi-mythical status and it is fair to say that Caesar was fortunate to be in a position to exploit the military developments of his predecessors. Great armies and great commanders are symbiotic – relying on each other. Caesar knew this and often publicly (though not always honestly) stated his respect for his troops: 'no condemnation could be too severe if Caesar did not hold the lives of his soldiers dearer than his own'.

The success of the Roman army was based on its ability to maintain long-term campaigns with a professional, disciplined and well-drilled force. While not great inventors themselves, Roman soldiers were unequalled at seizing upon the ideas of others and adapting them to their own needs. The heavy javelin, for example, as employed by Caesar's legions was cleverly designed so that its long, thin arrow-like head could easily penetrate shields and armour but would bend out of shape on impact so that it could not be thrown back.

Soldiers of the republican Roman army, from the frieze of the altar of the Temple of Neptune in Rome (Musee du Louvre).

The army was split between infantry and auxiliaries (non-Roman forces, including cavalry). Cavalry played a much lesser part than in Alexander's day, partly because Roman generals tended not to lead from the front with a cavalry charge straight at an opponent but, rather, to work more carefully by deploying the infantry units – the legions. Cavalry was used for reconnaissance, protection and pursuit but it was the legionaries who won or lost battles. The legionaries would charge at an enemy and, from about fifty feet (15m), throw their javelins. Each man then relied on his long, rectangular shield and a short thrusting-sword.

Units of eight men were the basic building block of the army and each of these units shared a tent. The Romans realized the importance of small units of men working together, forging a close relationship in which each man would rather fight than be seen to be scared, help his comrades in times of need, and work and suffer as part of a group rather than as an anonymous individual in a larger unit. To instil a feeling of loyalty to unit and army, great emphasis was often given to appearance. Caesar encouraged those of his men who could afford it to inlay their weapons with silver and gold; not only did this improve their appearance and encourage pride but it made the men very loath to drop their weapons in battle.

A legionary on campaign would carry a great deal of weight – fifty or sixty pounds (22 or 27kg) of baggage tied to a pole which he carried over his shoulder. Apart from the armour and weapons, he carried a few days' provisions, cooking instruments, an axe, instruments for entrenching and building camp, and a tool bag.

Roman attack was based on a secure defence. The soldiers were not only skilled fighters, but expert engineers who constructed camps, bridges and ships. In training they were taught not only to fight and march, but also how to build. At the end of each day, a campaigning army spent three or four hours building and supplying its camp. The men also had to repair their own clothes, and make their own tools. Without such skills not a man in Caesar's army would have returned home.

The backbone of the army were the centurions, who had risen up through the ranks to command a 'century' of about eighty men. Each legion had about sixty such 'centuries' led by centurions. They were the only professional officers and were tough, ruthless soldiers, cool and efficient in battle, hard and unforgiving in transit and camp. They were men who would hold their position against all the odds. Above them in seniority were the non-professional officers, the general staff, appointed by the general to command the legions or groups of legions on the battlefield or detached service. Caesar's loyal second-in-command Labienus, for example, was often sent to deal with ancillary problems. These men, though perhaps relatively experienced in military affairs, were generally ambitious politicians pursuing their own ends and liable to move on at any time.

Caesar was no innovator in the art or science of war, though he was a mighty exponent of both. He had read and informed himself of current military practices and his abilities stemmed from making the most out of what was available to him as he made his way through his new provinces. Napoleon believed that commanders in their forties were past their best. Caesar was forty-one and soon showed he was a match for anyone:

> Caesar was a most skilful swordsman and horseman, and showed surprising powers of endurance. He always led his army, more often on foot than in the saddle, went bareheaded in the sun and rain alike, and could travel for long distances at incredible speed in a gig, taking very little luggage. If he reached an unfordable river he would either swim or propel himself across it on an inflated skin; and often arrived at his destination before the messengers whom he had sent ahead to announce his approach.
>
> He judged his men by their fighting record, not by their morals or social position. Though turning a blind eye to much of their misbehaviour, and never laying down any fixed scale of penalties, he allowed no deserter or mutineer to escape severe punishment. Sometimes, if a victory had been complete enough, he relieved the troops of all military duties and let them carry on as wildly as they pleased. One of his boasts was: 'My soldiers fight just as well when they are stinking of perfume. (*Suetonius*)

Caesar's initial aim had been to conquer the wealthy lands to the north of Italy but a chance migration of a tribe called the Helvetii led him to redirect his attentions westwards – a move that was to change the course of European history.

The Helvetii had requested permission to cross Roman provincial land and resettle further to their west. Caesar deemed this unacceptable and refused; if he had allowed them to pass he would always have faced the possibility of an attack on his flank and lines of communication. The basis of his future conquests was the security of his supply lines and no potentially aggressive tribe could be allowed to threaten them. Caesar (referring to himself in the third person) wrote an account of the resulting battle:

> The Helvetii, with all their wagons, came after us. They deposited all their heavy baggage in one place, and then, fighting in very close order, drove back our cavalry and came on in a dense mass up to our front line.
>
> Caesar first of all had his own horse taken out of the way and then the horses of other officers. Caesar wanted the danger to be the same for everyone and for no one to have any hope of escape by flight. Then Caesar spoke a few words of encouragement to the men before joining battle.
>
> Hurling their javelins from above, our men easily broke up the enemy's mass formation and, having achieved this, drew their swords and charged. In fighting, the Gauls were seriously hampered because several of their overlapping shields were often pierced by a single javelin; the iron head would bend and they could neither get it out nor fight properly with their left arms. Many of them, after a number of vain efforts at disentangling themselves, preferred to drop their shields and fight with no protection for their bodies. In the end the wounds and the toil of battle were too much for them, and they began to retire to a hill about a mile (1.5km) away.

The battle was won by dogged pursuit and Caesar now saw the potential of continuing through Gaul. Caesar had learnt from Alexander the Great the power and usefulness of self-propaganda, and as his campaigns progressed he wrote a set of 'commentaries', beautifully written records that are the primary, almost solitary, account of his gradual conquest of Gaul. Caesar's concern was contemporary: to promote himself to the senators and general populace back in Rome. He wanted everyone to know just what he faced and how he dealt with his formidable opponents.

The Gauls were part of a Celtic-speaking people numbering many millions whose influence stretched from the British Isles to the Balkans. There was no central command over this vast area, rather a system of small kingdom states and tribes, associated in a constantly shifting mosaic of alliances. Gaul proper (roughly modern France and Belgium) was divided into about sixty such tribes, all dependent on agriculture and cattle-breeding. Some of these tribes were centred around sophisticated forts, others lived in small towns. The common people lived in a state of debt-bondage, ruled over by a warrior nobility.

Caesar saw the Gauls as semi-barbarians and it suited his political needs to portray them as such. Yet he also knew they possessed a well-developed culture and he certainly feared their renowned courage in battle. The Romans had conquered about half of Gaul by 60 BC but their influence in the northern areas was limited to trade (particularly of wine), along the roads and rivers. The Romans had been wary of the 'hairy Gauls' since they had sacked Rome some 300 years earlier, and despite some intermittent Roman victories, Gallic warriors, on the whole, scorned their Roman opponents.

Caesar intended to conquer Gaul by defeating the major tribes one by one. To achieve this goal he needed an army that could overcome such opposition. His first task, therefore, was to acquire – partly at his own expense – more troops, over and above those to which he was entitled to as governor. Crassus, Caesar's ally, is reported to have said: 'no man with political ambition is now sufficiently wealthy unless he can support an army on his own income.' Caesar, over the next few years, raised a force of ten legions – about 50,000 men as well as 10,000 to 20,000 allies, slaves and camp followers.

The key was to move gradually, defeating or making alliances with one tribe after another. Most important, and constantly referred to in Caesar's own writings, was the need to keep lines of supply and communication open. Although he was not always successful, he did try to make sure his routes back to stores and depots were kept free.

Caesar's first objective was to secure Gaul's eastern border along the Rhine. A former Roman ally, the German, Ariovistus, had crossed the Rhine and entered Caesar's Gallic domain. Caesar used this as the excuse he needed to provoke a confrontation. Caesar felt he had to explain to his men, especially his military commanders, why he was turning against Ariovistus and his experienced soldiers. The Germans may be allies now, he explained, but who knows what they might do in the future. Certainly the Germans had had their eye on Gaul for some time.

Roman soldiers engaged in battle with barbarians, from a sarcophagus in the National Museum, Rome.

Caesar manoeuvred himself around Ariovistus' flank. The enemy was superior in numbers, but the Romans had the edge in training and armour. Caesar had learnt that the Germans believed they would be defeated if they fought before the new moon, and so he forced battle upon them immediately. They were formidable foes but tended to run as a mob, scaring the Romans but not breaking the disciplined legions who held firm with their swords and javelins. The Germans were defeated and the Romans followed their victory with an appalling brutality against their enemy.

The following year, 57 BC, Caesar marched northwards against the Belgae, whose united tribes numbered many hundreds of thousands. The strength of the Roman army and Caesar's skills of persuasion and inducement brought the tribes under his rule.

Messengers were the lifeblood of Caesar's organization and he would sometimes use a secret code or write in Greek to communicate with his support staff of friends and colleagues. Yet, despite such preparations, Caesar was caught by surprise on more than one occasion. Part of the problem was his poor use of cavalry reconnaissance. Rome itself had no expertise in cavalry and Caesar, like other Roman generals, used foreign horsemen – particularly German and Celtic mercenaries. But he seems not to have trusted them with a larger role. Perhaps he did not come to grips with their potential for investigating what lay ahead of the marching armies. On campaign against the Nervii tribe, for example, he was completely taken by surprise when they swarmed down upon the marching Romans.

Under such pressure, however, Caesar showed the speed and resolution of action that elevated him above the ordinary commander. He was always the last person to show fear and could communicate this self-control to his troops. He was able to think and act calmly in the confusion and panic, and such cool behaviour maintained his men on an even keel, helping them to concentrate on exploiting their own skills and abilities. As long as the soldiers remained a coherent fighting body, there was little that could beat them. Against the Nervii, Caesar even fought in the front line. His great influence was to set an example to his soldiers.

The Romans suffered badly in this attack and it was only the knowledge that such a defeat would lead to their own massacre that made them fight fiercely enough to force the Nervii back. Caesar himself showed great personal bravery before the Nervii were finally broken and defeated. But it was poor reconnaissance that had brought him close to catastrophe.

As autumn ended, he returned to his winter quarters on the Italian borders, where he could meet with Romans and keep up with the latest developments and intrigues. Rome, for its part, was much impressed by his successes and staged a thanksgiving festival of fifteen days – the longest the Senate had ever granted.

The following year, 56 BC, Caesar returned to his provinces. Some of the Belgae had banded together again and a maritime tribe, the Veneti, had imprisoned a group of Romans searching for corn supplies. Caesar found it impossible to attack on land so he sent his fleet to deal with it. The Romans showed great ingenuity by attacking the enemy ships with knives mounted on long poles to slash sails and cut ropes. The immobilized navy was soon defeated and the survivors were, as usual, either sold into slavery or executed.

Caesar's cruelty has to be considered as bad politics as it served only to increase the animosity that the defeated tribes felt towards the Romans. He had chosen a path

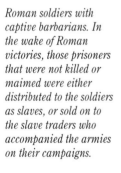

Roman soldiers with captive barbarians. In the wake of Roman victories, those prisoners that were not killed or maimed were either distributed to the soldiers as slaves, or sold on to the slave traders who accompanied the armies on their campaigns.

of total subjugation rather than integration and such a course was inevitably destined to be bloody and violent.

Caesar had now conquered many of the Gallic tribes and he began to look further afield. In 55 BC, after again defeating two German tribes who had crossed on to the western bank of the Rhine, Caesar – in defiance of Senate rules – became the first man to bridge the Rhine. This was an action as much to impress the Romans (whose support was so important to him) as to frighten the Germans. This flouting of Senate Law continued when he became the first Roman general to raid Britain. Although these two British raids were near-disasters and were later called 'second-rate' by Napoleon, from Caesar's point of view they were a great success. Once again, they impressed the ordinary people back in Rome and it was power in Rome that he ultimately sought: military command and the conquest of Gaul were merely means to an end. The following year, 54 BC, Caesar returned again to Britain, but it was a dismal sortie: many troops were killed in battle and many ships lost in a storm. Nevertheless, after the second raid Caesar received a huge twenty-day celebration in Rome. If his British ventures were military failures, they certainly proved to be propaganda successes.

> From Britain he had won nothing for himself or for the state except the glory of having conducted an expedition against its inhabitants; but on this he prided himself greatly and the Romans at home likewise magnified it to a remarkable degree. (*Dio*)

On his return from Britain in the autumn of 54 BC, Caesar faced a renewed revolt from the Belgae. The whole of the following year was spent in subduing the rebellion and ravaging the lands of those who had turned against him. In 52 BC, Caesar faced an even greater challenge. The tribes despised the way he treated them as a conquered people. Occupation by Caesar's forces had instilled a spirit of desperation in his enemies and the seperate tribes had finally come to an agreement between themselves. Under their leader, Vercingetorix, a talented prince from the Arveni, they committed themselves, once and for all, to defeating the Roman invaders.

Coin with the profile of the Gallic leader Vercingetorix.

Vercingetorix's first plan was simple but highly effective – strike at Caesar's supplies. Vercingetorix believed that as the harvest had been completed and everything was in stores, Caesar would have to send out foraging parties on raids. Vercingetorix was determined that not one of those parties would return. At the same time, he also persuaded his allies to burn their own villages and remaining crops. Caesar was to be left nothing and thus be starved out of Gaul.

Caesar had spent the winter in Cisalpine Gaul, near Italy, keeping in touch with friends and political allies. On learning of Vercingetorix's actions he hurried westward to join his armies. It took great skill and speed even to reach them as the Gauls had cut the lines of communications. Then, in immediate retaliation he attacked and defeated some of Vercingetorix's allies, overrunning and stripping settlement after settlement. One town, Gergovia, proved more resistant and Caesar was forced to lay siege. Having split his forces with his deputy Labienus who had marched against another tribe, the Parisii, Caesar had insufficient forces to complete the blockade. He

Battle between Roman and Gallic soldiers, from a frieze in the Ducal Palace at Mantua.

failed to take the town by storm and was forced to raise the siege for the only time in the Gallic campaign, and march to reunite his forces.

Vercingetorix and his now confident allies then made a fatal error. They switched from small-scale, guerilla tactics to direct confrontation. The attack the Gauls launched, however, failed against the reunited Roman forces and Vercingetorix was lucky to escape with most of his troops.

The Gauls retreated to Alesia, a town (north of modern Dijon in France) situated on a plateau about a mile (1.5km) long. The slopes up to the town were steep and unassailable and Vercingetorix felt perfectly safe. Having defeated Caesar in the previous siege, he was confident that he could do it again. But this time he underestimated his opponent.

Caesar had to consider what tactics he should use to defeat his Gallic enemy. Alesia's terrain made it impossible to attack and Caesar would either have to retreat

or lay siege. His overwhelming determination made the decision for him and he boldly decided to encircle the entire hill – a massive feat of engineering which the Romans had never undertaken on this scale before.

Caesar first established over twenty temporary bases around the hill to control the area and then began building his siege works and permanent camps. Between the two rivers, Ose and Oserain that pass Alesia, the Romans built a deep trench to prevent a surprise cavalry attack. Then around the hill they built two deep trenches about fifteen feet (5m) wide, the inner one of which was, where possible, flooded. Behind this, a twelve foot (4m) rampart of earth was crowned with a wooden defense with intermittent towers. This defence extended for about eleven miles (18km) around the hill. There were also four cavalry and four infantry camps. It was impossible for the Romans to defend the entire length so they installed elaborate and deadly obstacles. They used sharpened branches to make hedges of spikes. In front of these they dug

Alesia, in eastern France, where Caesar confronted the massed armies of the Gallic tribes gathered under the leadership of Vercingetorix. The town survives as modern-day Alice Ste. Reine.

rows of circular pits into which were embedded pointed stakes; these pits were then camouflaged with brushwood and twigs. In front of these they placed barbed metal spikes, sticking just out of the ground. The whole area must have been virtually deforested to provide the timber for such extensive workings. Caesar knew that Vercingetorix had sent for reinforcements and so he also ordered the construction of an outer defence line, fourteen miles (22km) long.

The inhabitants of Alesia must have looked on in wonder and fear. Vercingetorix had no idea how tenacious a Roman siege would be and was confident that he would soon receive the reinforcements that he had sent for. His mistake was to allow Caesar to build almost uninterrupted instead of taking control of nearby hills and forcing Caesar to over-extend his lines.

Vercingetorix was particularly concerned about feeding his troops. He sent out all those who could not fight, including women and children, and left them to the mercy of the Romans. Caesar, who had established his camp on a hill opposite Alesia, refused to allow them to pass through the lines and cause trouble or use up a portion of his supplies. These hapless townspeople were presumably stuck between the lines, and went hungry until the fighting was completed.

Vercingetorix's pleas for reinforcements were heeded – even tribes that Caesar had recently beaten and allied to Rome sent troops. Caesar estimated that 250,000 infantry and 8,000 cavalry arrived to confront him. Estimates such as these, then as now, are so often wildly inaccurate that it is hard to know how much credence to give them. However, since the Gauls were drawing from a population of between eight and twelve million, raising such a force would not have been impossible. The new troops set up camp on a hillside within sight of Caesar's own camp a mile (1.5km) away. Their cavalry was nearer, positioned on the three-mile-wide (5km) plain.

Faced with such overwhelming odds many leaders would have abandoned this position. Caesar, however, remained supremely confident in his and his troops' abilities. He reacted to the new arrivals by placing his own cavalry outside his lines facing his opponents. Vercingetorix's troops were greatly encouraged by the arrival of their allies and ran down to fill in the nearest trench, stimulating the new army (which had brought few supplies) to launch an immediate attack. Caesar lined up his infantry along the two lines of the entrenchments 'so that in case of need every man could know his post and hold it'. He then ordered his cavalry to charge the Gallic horsemen. The Gauls had placed archers and lightly-armed infantrymen in the ranks of their cavalry and these surprised Caesar's cavalry and forced them back. The Roman cavalry held on tenaciously for some hours until, at sunset, they assembled at one point and charged, forcing the Gauls to run back to their camp.

The following day, the main Gallic army waited until midnight before attacking – relying this time on their infantry to break down the defences. They worked fever-

The site of the unassailable fortress of Alesia, seen from Caesar's battlefield.

ishly to try and fill the trenches, and threw stones and arrows at the Romans on the ramparts, forcing some of them off. Vercingetorix was slow to see what was happening and was late marching out of the town; by the time he began attacking Caesar on the inner fortifications, the battle was almost over. Caesar had successfully relocated his troops to repel this attack with slingstones, large stones and javelins.

Many Gauls died on the hidden obstacles, falling onto the sharpened stakes or the metal spikes. By dawn they had pulled back. The Gauls had brought few supplies and Caesar had already stripped the surrounding countryside of food; they were forced to fight, starve or retreat. They decided to attempt an all-out assault on a Roman camp at the foot of Mount Reá to the north of Alesia. Approximately 60,000 infantry troops were sent at night, around the back of the hill. They arrived at dawn, rested out of sight until midday, and then launched their attack. At the same time the cavalry and the rest of the army attacked in front of their camp. Realizing what was happening, Vercingetorix astutely sent his troops to other points on the lines to draw off and split the Roman defences.

> Distributed as they were along lines of such length, the Romans found it difficult to meet simultaneous attacks in many different places. They were unnerved, too, by the shouts they could hear behind them as they fought . . . . It is nearly always invisible dangers that are most terrifying. (*Caesar*)

Caesar's situation was now critical: if the Gauls broke through, the Romans would be massacred. At first he watched and sent messages from his hill camp. From here he ordered his second-in-command, Labienus, to take 3,000 men to reinforce the 9,000 men trying to hold back the attack at Mount Reá. When it seemed necessary, however, Caesar mounted his horse and galloped to other parts of the line, encouraging his troops and telling them that all they had previously fought for depended on this day. The Gauls attacking on the plain had experienced mixed fortunes but had managed to pull down a part of the stockade. Caesar sent immediate relief troops, then more, and finally rushed to fight in person, until the attack was eventually repulsed.

Caesar now rushed to help Labienus who was experiencing great difficulty in holding off the Gauls at Reá. From a distance, Caesar summed up the situation in an instant and, without hesitation, sent all his reserve cavalry, especially his German mercenary horsemen, around the entrenchments and a nearby hill until they could surprise the Gauls from behind. Caesar himself then galloped to help Labienus. Over the years Caesar had increasingly commanded from further behind the front line, having decided that he usually stood to lose a great deal more by risking his life than he would gain by securing victory. This, however, was different: he would lose everything, including his life, if he lost at Alesia.

Once they saw the scarlet cloak of their commander-in-chief, the Romans, who according to Caesar had been beginning to tire, raised a cheer, dropped or threw their last javelins and began to fight hand-to-hand with swords. Those few who held

back, or worse, tried to run away, were grabbed by the throat and forced back (some-times by Caesar himself) to face the enemy again.

The view across the plain below Alesia.

When Caesar's horsemen appeared to their rear, the Gauls panicked and the retreating, disorganized army was easy prey. The entire Gallic relief army, realizing that their great plan had failed, fled, but the Romans were too exhausted to give chase.

Vercingetorix saw that he was defeated and, the following day, surrendered in person. The battle of Alesia was over: Caesar had successfully defended twenty-five miles (40km) of entrenchment, an enormous distance, and, outnumbered by perhaps as much as five to one, had beaten two armies.

Caesar did not treat Vercingetorix as Alexander had treated King Porus. This defeated general was offered no pity; he was chained up like an animal and led off to be paraded through the streets of Rome, where Romans would see what the 'Great Caesar' had captured, fought and beaten. Vercingetorix's fate was sealed and he was later ritually strangled during Caesar's 'Triumph of Gaul' parade through Rome. Had Caesar been more magnanimous in victory, it might not have taken him nine years to conquer Gaul.

Nor were the defeated inhabitants of Alesia and captured Gallic soldiers treated much better. They were distributed one apiece to the soldiers, who either kept them to help carry baggage or sold them to the slave-traders that accompanied the army.

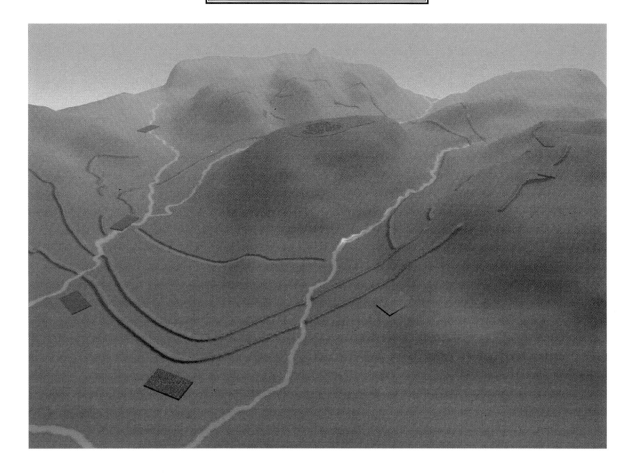

Caesar's fortifications and encampments (in blue) surrounding the Gallic stronghold of Alesia.

In 51 BC, the year after the battle of Alesia, some Gallic tribes made one final attempt to evict the Romans from their lands but failed. Caesar assembled all the Gallic tribal chiefs and demanded their alliance to Rome. They were too weak to refuse and Caesar's strength, flattery, bribery and uncompromising behaviour left them no choice but to agree. Gaul was now secured as a Roman province.

Caesar had brought a large new area under Roman control which was to change the focus of Rome from the Mediterranean to western Europe. Sullen in defeat, the tribes of Gaul accepted Rome as their master. The fighting prowess and dogged determination of the Roman armies and of Caesar himself had broken them.

Caesar was now determined to take executive power in Rome itself; as he was not to be granted it legally, he decided to take it illegally. He and his battle-hardened armies crossed the River Rubicon – the border to Italy – and marched on Rome, thus declaring war on their own state.

> . . . when I notice how carefully arranged his hair is and when I watch him adjusting his parting with one finger, I cannot imagine that this man could conceive of such a wicked thing as to destroy the Roman Constitution. (*Cicero*)

Rome was in a panic: the whole edifice of political leadership was under threat and only one man could stop Caesar – his old ally Pompey. Pompey was an excellent general but he lacked the political insight and the cold ruthlessness of Caesar. Although the two armies were Roman, Caesar held the advantage of knowing why he was fighting: he had a clear grand strategy. He also had the advantage of fighting with veterans, whereas Pompey's armies were hastily reconstructed from retired soldiers and new recruits.

Pompey withdrew from Italy to gain time to train his troops. Caesar tried to stop him but failed. After a number of setbacks which he overcame through sheer determination, he finally defeated Pompey in Greece. Pompey then fled to Egypt, but he was murdered by the young Egyptian boy-king, Ptolemy XII. Caesar was now clearly master of Rome and thus of much of the western world. Yet he did not return immediately to Rome. First, he spent some time with his new mistress, Ptolemy's sister, Cleopatra, whom Caesar made Queen of Egypt. Then, in August, 47 BC, he beat a hostile king in Asia Minor (where Caesar uttered the immortal words 'veni, vidi, vici', – 'I came, I saw, I conquered'). The hesitation before returning home had allowed Pompey's sons to raise new armies and Caesar had to fight again in northern Africa; finally, in March, 45 BC, in one great battle in Spain, he defeated the last remnants of bitter opposition.

Reconstruction of the pallisades and towers built by the Romans at Alesia.

Rome was exhausted by the stresses of civil war and realized that only Caesar offered the chance of relief and maybe even recuperation. He was offered, and accepted, a 'dictatorship' – a six-month office of one-man rule used in emergencies. On his return, he paid off his army with gold and farms, and laid on huge victory celebrations. Four hundred lions were hunted to death in the circus, a naval battle was held on a specially flooded campus and, as a grand finale, two armies of war captives and criminals fought each other to the death. To those soldiers and senators whom he had defeated he, for once, showed noticeable clemency. Caesar knew the value of high-profile mercy and the accompanying favours-in-hand it provided him for a later date. Much to Caesar's surprise, some Romans refused to join in the festivities; they questioned the cost and whether the defeat of a Roman army was cause for celebration. Worse dissent followed when Caesar brought a foreign queen, his mistress Cleopatra, and their son Caesarion from Egypt to Rome. People feared that Caesar was beginning to consider himself a king. Nevertheless, he was still able to manipu-

Gladiators in combat with wild animals. Gladiators were specially trained slaves who fought each other or fierce animals for the entertainment of Roman citizens. It was thought fitting that the population should be accustomed to the sight of death.

Bust of Cicero.

late the supercilious Senate in to declaring him dictator for life. He had finally fulfilled his ambition of becoming the autocratic leader of the Roman world.

Although Caesar introduced some measures to improve general living conditions, he was equally concerned with erecting huge monuments – temples, libraries and canals – to his reign. His reforms of the calender, which lengthened the year from 355 to 365 days a year, with an added day every four years, have survived to this day; as has the month of July, the name having been changed by the Senate in honour of their great Caesar. (The Emperor Augustus later copied Caesar and introduced August.)

Caesar crowned with a wreath of laurel.

Caesar imposed tariffs on foreign goods, cracked down on luxuries, and hoped to reduce the Civil Code to manageable proportions. It is said that he also intended to establish grandiose public schemes, such as improving drainage and roads. But these schemes never saw the light of day. At the age of fifty-five, he was assassinated.

Why was he killed not in battle but in Rome by fellow politicians? Rome needed a strong, individual leader but the hatred of monarchy was still strong, especially within the upper classes who preferred a system in which they could all share a slice of power. Now, as Cicero pointed out, 'All power has been placed in the hands of one man' and that left little opportunity for ambitious senators. For the more idealistic,

Ruins of the room behind the theatre of Pompey in Rome in which Caesar was murdered. The room was being used for Senatorial meetings during reconstruction of the Senate House.

this quasi-monarchy was everything republican Rome was opposed to. Even having a queen in Rome seemed to confer 'kingship' on Caesar, which further twisted the knife in the Republic's back. The Republic was on its last legs because it had not been able to create the institutions to deal with the vastly increased wealth and influence that successful conquest had brought. Agricultural labourers and landowners had joined the army and left their homes and farms to be run by the increasing numbers of slaves. Rome's own economy eventually shrank until only the fruits of occupation kept the system afloat. The subsequent corruption had thoroughly rotted the administration. Perhaps Caesar's one-man rule was just what Rome needed to survive, but the ruling class would not accept the loss of their own status. A system based on patronage depends on the ability to deliver the favours required of it. This was threatened by one-man rule.

On 18 March, 44 BC, Caesar planned to leave Rome and begin a campaign in the east. It was a strange intention, as much was left unfinished in Rome and such a cam-

Bust of Caesar from the Museo Nazionale, Napoli. After his death Caesar, whose family claimed descent from the goddess Venus, was himself declared a god, and a temple dedicated to his worship was erected in the forum in Rome.

paign would keep him away for two or three years. Perhaps he saw himself as the new Alexander the Great. Maybe he needed the coarse humour and honesty of his soldiers and wanted to be free of the musty intrigues of Rome. There is a crucial difference between the acquisition of power and its execution; Caesar may have discovered that he preferred the former. In his absence, some of Caesar's allies were to govern Rome and that also inflamed senatorial passions. Enough was enough – Caesar had to be removed.

Caesar was apparently unconcerned by threats on his life. Perhaps he felt so empowered that he feared no one. Perhaps he became sick or tired. Maybe he simply wanted to be king, even for a short while. He was also a brave man. When recommended to maintain a bodyguard he declined, saying: 'It is better to die once than live always in the fear of death'.

On the Ides of March, three days before he was due to leave on campaign, the great general who had fought in so many foreign lands was killed in Rome, in a small room behind the Theatre of Pompey, stabbed twenty-three times by fellow senators.

Rome was thrown into chaos. Caesar's nineteen-year-old grandnephew Octavian, (later called Augustus) had apparently been adopted in Caesar's will (in preference to Caesar's only son, the young Caesarion) and initially he and Mark Anthony took over the reins of power. To prevent any likelihood of Caesarion threatening his power, Augustus had him killed. By 31 BC, Augustus ruled alone. After the period of kings and then the republic, the third and final stage of the classical history of Rome had begun – that of the emperors.

The conquest of Gaul, secured by the victory of Alesia, changed the face of Europe, accelerating the decline of the Celtic-speaking world and opening up western and central Europe to Mediterranean civilization. It was a turning-point in history, but for Caesar it was little more than a stepping-stone to his ultimate desire: control of Rome. Caesar was, from start to finish, a manipulator governed by ambition. The ultimate weapon, war, was an instrument of policy.

And, as with all great commanders, he was well served by luck. As his 'luck' increased so did the air of the supernatural around him. If he were blessed, thought the soldiers, then they too could benefit from the benevolence of the gods.

In pursuit of self-advancement, Caesar was prepared to brush aside constitutional obstacles in the belief that he, and only he, could save the Roman state from itself. He was little interested in establishing a personal dynasty but instead wanted to be respected and loved as a great leader in his own lifetime. However, while Rome was willing to accept him as a great commander, it would not accept him as its king.

Tactically he made mistakes but strategically he almost always out-performed his opponents. His personal intervention, backed by his self-belief, and that crucial slice of good fortune always turned the tide in his favour. Caesar also had two great advantages that have helped his legend survive: he wrote one of the very few accounts of a Roman military commander's campaigns. Naturally enough, these accounts serve to convince the reader of Caesar's skills. And he was also the first man to conquer great swathes of Europe; in the process both bridging the Rhine and invading Britain. Julius Caesar's career as politician and military commander left deep and long-lasting scars on European consciousness – scars that persist to this day.

CHAPTER THREE

HORATIO NELSON

'The greatest and most simple of men.' (Alexander Scott)

He was vain, ambitious, disfigured by battle, adulterous, and almost wrecked by a life at sea. He disobeyed orders, made up his own rules and was pensioned off for five years. Nevertheless, every 21 October, on British naval bases and warships throughout the world, glasses are raised to 'the immortal memory' of Horatio Nelson. For good or ill, it is Nelson who symbolizes the devotion to country, military ability, humour, courage, sacrifice and greed that lay at the heart of the British Empire.

Nelson sailed the world, fighting engagement after engagement for his country, seeking both success for his nation and glory for himself. His skills as a sailor and commander established Britain's maritime supremacy, and his final battle, Trafalgar, not only ended French hopes of invading Britain, but also secured a domination at sea that allowed for the establishment of a powerful empire.

Nelson's roots offer little indication that he was destined for such a future. He was born on 29 September 1758, one of eleven children of the Reverend Edmund Nelson and his wife Catherine. The family lived in a rural village called Burnham Thorpe, in the English county of Norfolk.

At night, from the garden of their home, the Parsonage, Nelson could hear the waves breaking on the nearby seashore. Although a small and somewhat frail boy, he would often walk the two miles (3km) to the local harbour to watch the tide rolling in, the traders unloading their wares, the ships heading towards imagined adventures. This was an age of discovery and adventure and Nelson's head was full of the romance of life at sea. Horatio's uncle, Maurice Suckling, was a naval captain with victories to his credit and it was he that Horatio hoped one day to emulate.

Edmund Nelson used his position and small income to secure his sons as good an education as possible and Horatio was sent away to boarding school. During

Horatio Nelson as a young post captain, painted between 1777 and 1781 by Francis Rigaud. Nelson was still a lieutenant when the painting was begun, the painter was forced to make a series of changes to the uniform to keep up with his subject's rapid promotion.

The rectory at Burnham Thorpe where Nelson was born and which remained his home during the early years of his marriage.

Christmas 1767, both Horatio's grandmother and mother died. For the sensitive Horatio, this proved to be extremely upsetting. Precociously, the nine year old declared himself willing and ready to go to sea 'to provide for himself'. His father, unconvinced, sent him back to school.

Although Nelson wanted to join the navy, there would have been little opportunity to do so. Britain at this time was at peace and therefore the Royal Navy ships were largely 'in Ordinary' (in reserve) with their masts and rigging removed and only a few officers looking after them. The sailors had been paid off and were looking for alternative work. In 1770, however, the Spanish invaded the Falkland Islands, a British territory in the southern Atlantic, and a force was hurriedly assembled to sail south. Horatio's uncle was among those appointed a command and the young Nelson persuaded his father to ask him for a place on board. Uncle Maurice replied:

> What has poor Horatio done, who is so weak, that he should be sent to rough it out at sea? But let him come, and the first time we go into action a cannon ball may knock off his head and provide for him at once.

Nelson left Norfolk early in 1771 and journeyed to Chatham docks, on the River Medway, east of London. Once he had arrived he wandered disconsolately through the harbourside noise and confusion, looking in childish wonder at the great wooden ships. Eventually he made his way aboard his uncle's ship and was taken below decks to the cramped space where he was to sling his hammock. Nelson had begun his sea career.

Life on board one of His Majesty's ships was tough and unforgiving. Horatio was one of hundreds sleeping in dark, damp, stinking spaces, working long hours and pushed to their physical limits. The food was generally awful and the water often so bad that few drank it. One of Horatio's peers wrote: 'We live on beef which quite makes your throat cold in eating it, owing to the maggots which are very cold when you eat them, like calves' foot jelly or blomonge (sic), being very fat indeed.' Beer and wine were therefore often the saving grace of life at sea. One captain reported: 'In hot climates, I really do not think it an exaggeration to say that one-third of every ship's company were more or less intoxicated.'

This captain was exaggerating: the punishment for drunkenness at sea was flogging and most preferred to save their bacchanalian release until they were in harbour, when whole ships' companies were known to get totally drunk. Often the crews' behaviour depended on how much they had been paid and that, in turn, could depend on how many enemy ships they had captured and how generous the prize court and the captain had been when sharing out the booty.

Life on board was a strictly regulated hierarchy of command and control. Faced with months, even years, without disembarking, every privilege was carefully monitored, every relationship delicately balanced. At the centre of this tangled web stood the captain. He was not only the commander but also judge and jury, and far from home it was up to the captain to make autonomous decisions. To punish his men, a captain could order twelve lashes without referring to a senior for confirmation.

Seamen in Nelson's time were often considered a race apart from the ordinary population: theirs was a way of life that passed through generations and the men shared a distinct culture and language. On warships much of the crew was made up of merchant seamen coerced into the sevice of the Royal Navy by press gangs.

More severe punishment was supposed to be put before a committee or court martial of captains or even the Admiralty itself. Such regulations were often ignored, except where capital punishment was concerned. Sailors had no objection to this as long as they were treated fairly; what they hated were tyrannical, irrational or slack captains and officers – of which the British Navy had its fair share.

The twelve-year-old Nelson had all the rigours of navy life before him. The Falklands dispute, however, was resolved diplomatically before the fleet was called into action. Fortunately for Nelson, his uncle had been struck by his nephew's enthusiasm and arranged for his transfer to a merchant ship heading to the West Indies. Suckling's appointment paid dividends and gave Nelson an outsider's view of the Royal Navy which proved invaluable over the years to come. He also proved himself a good seaman. In 1773 Nelson exploited his uncle's contacts once again to leave the merchant navy and travel on a scientific survey to the Arctic. The mission itself was not a success but Nelson was again noted for his confidence and determination. On his return, now aged fifteen, he sailed to India, a journey he thoroughly enjoyed until he was struck down with malaria and repatriated. Once recovered, his thirst for travel remained unquenched and, back in England, unsure what his future should be, he sank into a depression. During this period, Nelson found solace in a vision that his destiny was to be a national hero; Britain's industrial expansion and the need to protect trade with its expanding empire would provide him with the opportunity to fulfil this vision.

Nelson first saw action as a lieutenant in 1776, during the American War of Independence. The war gave Nelson the opportunity he had been waiting for to demonstrate his courage. During a gale, his own ship captured an American vessel:

> The first Lieutenant was ordered to board her, which he did not do, owing to the very heavy sea. On his return, the Captain said, 'Have I no Officer in the Ship who can board the Prize?' On which the Master ran to the gangway, to get into the boat: when I stopped him, saying, 'It is my turn now' . . . difficulties and dangers do but increase my desire of attempting them. (*Nelson*)

In December 1778, he was promoted to captain and given command of the ship *Badger*, which was sent to protect British trade in the Honduras from American private ships. Success at this venture led, at the age of only twenty, to promotion to post-captain – a rank that meant he could be appointed to one of the large warships. As long as he avoided death or disgrace (which many captains failed to do) he could now expect automatic promotion, eventually to admiral.

With the end of the war in 1783, however, Nelson, like thousands of others, was relieved of duties and ordered home on half-pay. He travelled to France – to learn the language of the 'enemy' – but found it 'full of English, I suppose because the wine is so very cheap' and he soon returned home. He then tried, but failed, to get into Parliament. Just when things were looking black, he received notification that he was to be given command of a ship bound for the West Indies.

While there, Nelson was assigned to escort the King's son, Prince William, and sail with him. He accompanied the Prince to parties by night and sailing by day, discussing naval actions of the past. Prince William, later King William IV, remembered Nelson thus:

> Captain Nelson . . . appeared to be the merest boy of a Captain I ever beheld . . . . There was something irresistibly pleasing in his address and conversation; and an enthusiasm, when speaking on professional subjects, that showed he was no common being.

During this period, Nelson married Frances Nisbet (a widow with one child). Prince William gave the bride away and noted that Nelson looked sick with nervousness and 'more in need of a nurse than a bride'.

After his return from the West Indies, Nelson waited despairingly in Norfolk for five years for his country to call upon his services. But Britain was at peace, and as long as the fragile balance in Europe held – not least because the old enemy France was at first too preoccupied with revolution to consider going to war – the country had little need of military commanders. Nelson also suffered from his own punctilious approach to naval matters. Ironically, had he been less stern about maintaining British naval law abroad or preventing petty corruption, his career might have advanced more quickly. Nevertheless, in early 1793, the expansionist aspirations of the new French Republic led it to declare war on Britain and Holland. Nelson was recalled to active service.

The church at Burnham Thorpe, where Nelson's father was rector. Nelson was forced to return to the small Norfolk village for a long period on half pay while Britain was at peace and much of its navy laid up.

This was a period of continual skirmishing, conducted with great energy by both sides, and particularly in the Mediterranean, where Nelson was sent to help defend and consolidate British-controlled ports. Unlike Alexander or Caesar, Nelson operated under the direct authority of others, and at times he did not grasp his superiors's wider strategic aims. His understanding of local objectives was, in comparison, flawless. In early 1795, for instance, Nelson helped take the island of Corsica in the face of heavy opposition, realizing the importance of the island and its ready stock of raw materials: 'The pine of this Island is of the finest texture I ever saw.'

It was during the action to take Corsica that Nelson's right eye was severely damaged by sand and debris when a cannonball hit a sandbag near where he was standing. His vision was badly impaired, necessitating the use of a green sun-shade above his eyes to protect them from strong glare.

By 1796, France, recently allied with Spain, dominated Europe. The British economy was suffering in the face of war-debts, and some of its Navy had mutinied due to harsh conditions and the callous behaviour of certain captains. The British Government, to Nelson's despair, decided that the Mediterranean could no longer be maintained and the fleet was to leave immediately. In no position to disobey, Nelson sailed west past Gibraltar early in 1797. As fate would have it, he sailed in fog straight into the Spanish fleet. He passed through the enemy fleet and hastened to his superior, Jervis, who needed little persuading that the Spanish must be attacked.

The battle was fought just off Cape St Vincent, at the south-western corner of Portugal, on St Valentines Day (14 February) 1797, with fifteen British ships opposing twenty-seven Spanish. Jervis, on his ship *Victory*, gave the orders and Nelson on board his ship *Captain* waited in anticipation for the signal to engage. The naval doctrine captains were expected to adhere to was set out in the navy's 'fighting instructions'. One of the key elements was that ships fought in a line, sideways on to the enemy and firing cannon straight at them.

Jervis sailed for the gap between the two divisions, hoping to divide the enemy ships and then turn to attack the larger of the two groups. Nelson spotted from his position that Jervis' leading ships would not have time to turn in succession and achieve this, so, without orders, he sailed out of British line and straight for the enemy.

This action was less reckless than might be imagined: he knew the Spanish were badly trained and lacked battle experience, and that their rate of fire would thus be well below the British equivalent. Nelson's attack thoroughly disconcerted the Spanish but he was still in an extremely dangerous position – initially sailing alone, his seventy-four guns faced many hundreds – and the Spaniards had soon all but wrecked his ship, having in the course of an hour shot away most of her sails and rigging, leaving her unable to manoeuvre. Resolve is an element of great command and Nelson managed to continue forward regardless, and rammed the Spanish ship, *San Nicolas*, which in the confusion had become entangled with another, the Spanish *San Josef*.

A soldier of the 69th Regiment having broke the upper quarter-gallery window, jumped in, followed by myself and others, as fast as possible. I found the cabin doors fastened and the Spanish officers fired their pistols at us through the windows, but, having broke open the doors . . . I found . . . the Spanish ensign hauling down. (*Nelson*)

A thirty-pounder cannon in action. When a shot was fired the cannon could recoil up to twenty feet under the force of the blast. Horrific injuries due to being caught in its path were common in the confusion of battle.

Both ships's crews had little inclination to fight hand-to-hand and Nelson proudly accepted their surrender. Nelson's ship had not, of course, been the only ship involved but it was he who took the glory for the battle's successful outcome. Within the fleet, tales of his action became legendary: word spread of 'Nelson's New Art of Cookery':

Take a Spanish . . . ship and after well battering and basting them for an hour, keep throwing in your force balls and be sure to let these be well seasoned. Your fire must never slacken for a moment, but must be kept up as brisk as possible during the whole time. So soon as you perceive your Spaniards to be well stewed and blended together, you must throw your own ship on the two-decker . . . skip in to her quarter-gallery window, sword in hand. The moment that you appear . . . the Spaniards will all throw down their arms and fly. [It] may now be considered as completely dished and fit to be set before His Majesty.

As ships' guns could be fired only to the side, naval battles most often took the form of stationary confrontations between opposing fleets deployed in parallel lines.

This action was typical of Nelson's courage and flair for independent action. One fellow captain described his leaving the line to attack the Spanish in this manner as a 'piece of individual initiative . . . unsurpassed in naval history'.

In July of the same year, Nelson, now knighted and a rear-admiral, led a landing at Tenerife. Admirals were not supposed to place themselves at such risk as their loss would severely disrupt the command hierarchy. During the attack, Nelson was hit in the right arm, which had to be amputated near the shoulder. Displaying a feeling towards fellow sailors that was already such an important part of his character he subsequently ordered that the surgeons always heat their blades before performing such operations: the cold knife had felt dreadful. Sedated with opium, Nelson returned to England for the first time in four and a half years. The young energetic man that had left Norfolk in 1793 returned a half-blind, semi-crippled, drug-sedated wreck. Neither Nelson nor his wife imagined that he would return to sea: 'a left-handed Admiral will never again be considered as useful'.

Remarkably, within a few months, Nelson – despite his injuries and self-pity, which were both expertly cared for by his wife – was back at sea, hunting in vain for the French Toulon fleet. For weeks he searched the Mediterranean until at last, at noon on 1 August 1798, he found them, sheltering in Aboukir Bay off the Egyptian coast – the setting for Nelson's first great battle as commander.

Napoleon had landed an army in Egypt and was intending to take over British trade routes to the east. By smashing the French fleet, Nelson hoped to crush such ambitions. Once the two fleets saw each other Nelson guessed that the last thing the French would expect would be an immediate night attack. The French, for their part, felt confident that their anchorage in the crescent-shaped bay afforded them almost complete protection and that they could pick off the British ships one by one as they approached. Failing that, they would sail out to fight them the following day and defeat them with their superior firepower. Nelson, however, had decided to attack straight away and catch the French by surprise. As some of the French sailors were on land gathering water this proved to be the right course of action. Nelson and his captains were ready for battle:

> With the masterly ideas of the Admiral, therefore, on the subject of Naval tactics, every one of the Captains of his Squadron was most thoroughly acquainted; and upon surveying the situation of the Enemy, they could ascertain with precision what were the ideas and intentions of the Commander, without the aid of any further instructions. (*Sir Edmund Berry*)

The battle began just after sunset, with only the stars, the phosphorescent waves and gun flashes to illuminate the scene. During the first two hours the British gained superiority over, and defeated, the leading ships of the French line. As they turned their attention to the middle of the line, Nelson was grazed on the forehead by shrapnel. Melodramatic as always, he exclaimed: 'I am killed, remember me to my wife.' In fact he was only concussed and was taken below decks. At 10 p.m. the French Admiral's huge ship *l'Orient* exploded, and by midnight the battle at the middle of the line had been won. By dawn the end of the French line also lay shattered. Of thirteen French ships that had sheltered in the bay the night before, ten had been captured (six of which were later incorporated into the British fleet), two had escaped

Cartoon of Nelson as 'The British Hero cleansing the Mouth of the Nile'. His victories aroused great patriotic fervour at a time when the British felt increasingly under threat from their continental opponents.

*Miniature of Emma,
Lady Hamilton, from
an original portrait by
Vigee le Brun thought to
be one of the truest like-
nesses. Emma's hopes of
being presented at court
in England were dashed
by the scandal of her
affair with Nelson, news
of which had reached
London before their
return. With typical
vanity, Nelson was
more worried that the
Prince of Wales would
turn his attentions
towards his beloved.*

and one was a wreck. 'Victory', said Nelson, 'is not a name strong enough for such a scene.' Nelson himself was dubbed the 'Hero of the Nile' and the commemorative cup and plate industry in Britain made a fortune.

Among Nelson's admirers was the King of Naples who created him Nelson Duke of Bronte (which means thunder). In England, his fame spread rapidly, and the new 'Duke of Bronte' stimulated an enormous following. This included a Yorkshireman called Brunty who changed his family name to Bronte and consequently the novels of his daughters became those of the Bronte sisters.

After the victory, Nelson was seduced by the image of his own heroism. His behaviour embarrassed almost all who knew him. The Sultan of Turkey gave him

several presents, including a diamond spray with a clockwork rotating star in the middle – Nelson loved it but his captains had to hide their amusement behind their handkerchiefs.

Nelson was upset that he had not been made commander-in-chief of the Mediterranean fleet and his attentions turned increasingly to his mistress Emma Hamilton – a once great beauty married to the British Ambassador in Naples. Although not universally admired and considered coarse and ill-mannered by some, Nelson fell deeply in love with her and was happy for the world to know it. It was this type of down-to-earth emotional display that so endeared him to his sailors. He never claimed to be a better man than they; he too could fall in love with a large, vulgar, married woman whose past was, in society's view, tainted. In January 1801, in England, she gave birth to a daughter, named, perhaps unsurprisingly, Horatia.

In 1801, the British faced the possibility of new foes – Scandinavia and Russia. In the face of Napoleon's expanding power, supplies from abroad were becoming increasingly difficult to secure. These shortages affected industrial growth – not least for the Navy itself, which relied on foreign timber, hemp and other raw materials to build and furnish its ships. Napoleon had sought an alliance with Russia, Sweden and Denmark (which included Norway) and if that alliance were allowed to go ahead, supplies to Britain would have been even further diminished. Early in the spring of 1801 the fleet was sent to launch a pre-emptive blow against Denmark to prevent her alliance with France. The opposing fleets lined up against each other in the waters just outside of Copenhagen, and engaged in a bloody battle that Nelson, recently promoted to vice-admiral, called the most terrible engagement he had been in. At one stage, his commander-in-chief, Admiral Sir Hyde Parker, had sent the order to 'leave off action'. When Nelson was told about this command he responded by placing the telescope to his blind right eye and declared: 'I have only one eye. I have a right to be blind sometimes. I really do not see the signal.'

No military organization can sustain such disregard for orders, but in this instance Nelson's courage won the day, and he went in person into Copenhagen to negotiate the armistice. In the face of such success, few dared or felt motivated to criticize him. Defeat, on the other hand, would no doubt have brought him into direct confrontation with his superiors in London.

It was clear that Napoleon was now intending to invade Britain itself, and Nelson was put in charge of anti-invasion forces. This involved travelling the country making speeches to volunteers and putting the general public's minds at rest. In August of 1801, he went back to sea and launched a pre-emptive strike against French vessels in Boulogne – only to be soundly beaten. Some of his heroic sheen was tarnished and posters went up warning sailors that life with Nelson meant being butchered at the earliest opportunity.

In May 1803, after a brief period of peace, Nelson was recalled, and made commander-in-chief of the Mediterranean fleet. His task was to keep track of the French and engage them whenever possible. As commander-in-chief he no longer captained an

Contemporary aquatint of action at the battle of Copenhagen. The battle was an almost static confrontation in which the superior training and experience of the British gunners proved largely responsible for the victory.

individual ship but sailed on an appointed flagship, in this case, the *Victory*, commanded by Thomas Hardy. This 100-gun ship was one of the finest ships in the navy. The crew of eight hundred, (only one-third volunteers) were mainly English, with a good many Scots, Irish and Welsh. The remainder were foreigners of many nationalities, including Americans and Frenchmen. Most of the crew were aged between twenty and thirty, and only a few dozen were over forty; the youngest, the servant boys, were not even in their teens.

Keeping the French fleet in their ports was tedious work, but no invasion could be launched while the Mediterranean and the English Channel were patrolled.

Nelson was sent to watch over the French Admiral Villeneuve's fleet at Toulon. His endurance during this period was quite remarkable. For eighteen months he sailed back and forth outside the port, making sure that Villeneuve could not set sail. In the middle of January 1805, however, the French fleet took advantage of a gale, which had pushed Nelson away from Toulon, and slipped out towards the Atlantic.

Although he was supposed to stay within European waters, Nelson gave chase and followed Villeneuve all the way to the Caribbean. Nelson wrote to a colleague: 'None of us would wish for exactly a West India trip; but the call of our Country is far superior to any consideration of self.'

Napoleon's plan was to draw British ships away from Europe. It was intended that Nelson would chase Villeneuve who, having drawn Nelson all the way to the Caribbean, would suddenly turn and rush back to the Channel to protect the flotilla of ships that could then transport the French army to Britain. Nelson acted as hoped, but he assumed, correctly, that the Channel would be protected by other British ships.

Nelson travelled approximately 100 miles (160km) a day for seventy days, crossing the Atlantic without a sight of the enemy. On 20 July 1805, Nelson returned to Europe and finally went ashore at Gibraltar for the first time since 16 June 1803. He was utterly exhausted. Two days later, another British admiral was more fortunate and confronted Villeneuve's elusive French fleet heading towards the northern Spanish coast. Admiral Calder, however, was no Nelson and broke off the engagement. The skirmish and capture of two enemy ships would once have earned him acclaim but Nelson had changed people's expectations. Only total victory, the destruction and capture of the opponent's fleet, was now good enough. Calder was later court-martialled for his actions.

On 18 August, a despondent and tired Nelson arrived back at his home in Merton (the house he shared with Emma Hamilton and her benevolent husband) for a brief period of recovery. Although he felt that he had failed, his country saw it differently and he was fêted wherever he was seen – and, of course, his disabilities meant that he was always recognized. Indeed, one of the reasons that Nelson became a 'great commander' is that he was so visible. He was an easy symbol for the population to latch on to and naturally, in times of such great stress, put their exaggerated faith in. Admiral Cornwallis, who played a crucial part by continually patrolling the Channel to deter any invasion, was, by comparison, no publicity seeker, his successes were more subtle and he had nothing distinguishable about his features; although he was a fine and efficient admiral, he has all but been forgotten.

On 20 August, it was reported that the French under Villeneuve, together with the Spanish under Gravina, had sailed to the southern Spanish port of Cadiz. The British set out to control and, it was hoped, to destroy them.

Trafalgar is certainly the most famous British naval battle ever fought. Not only has it entered British cultural mythology in a way that few other battles have – and the responsibility for this lies predominantly with Nelson himself – but it is of great historical importance, securing the control of the seas that greatly contributed to the growth of Britain's empire.

Early in September 1805 – after less than a month at home – Nelson was recalled to command the fleet, sailing again with *Victory* (still under Captain Hardy) as his flagship. Patrolling the seas was stretching the British fleet to its limits, as Napoleon hoped it would, and if no decisive battle was precipitated British endurance might break, allowing the French to invade. Nelson had to move quickly once he reached the fleet on 28 September.

Looking out to sea from Cape Trafalgar.

Nelson knew the benefits of meticulous preparation and first made sure that his troops were well supplied with meat, fruit and water. Although he had only thirty-three ships and feared the enemy had forty he was willing to send six ships to Gibraltar and Tangiers to buy stores, telling his intermediaries not to be 'penny wise and pounds foolish'. Then he had to prepare his captains. His officers had given him the 'sweetest reception of his life', and were now eager to hear his plans. They respected his personality and intelligence as much as his understanding of warfare. Once, when frustrated by the slow, methodical workings of the British army at Corsica, Nelson had written 'My disposition cannot bear tame and slow measures . . . I cannot help feeling a happy degree of irregularity is sometimes better than all this regularity.' Nelson's tactics at Trafalgar reflect this attitude: they were simple, adventurous, and based on opportunity and trust. His subordinates were to know the plan so thoroughly that they could act on their own initiative. Nelson and his 'Band of Brothers' (his fellow captains at sea) would spend hours discussing tactics and strategy until all knew instinctively what to do. Like any sea battle, once it had begun there was relatively little that the commander could do.

Nelson held two dinners on consecutive nights to go over his plans again with his captains. As a final instruction, Nelson, knowing that in battle smoke and wood-dust would obscure his signals, told his officers: 'No captain can do very wrong if he places his ship alongside that of an enemy.'

Nelson's early years working below decks had provided him with a wealth of technical ability that many officers who had entered at command level lacked.

Nelson understood his ships and what they were capable of: he was fully aware of the range of armaments and rates of fire for each ship in his fleet. Generally, the British aimed at the hulls of the enemy ships to try to destroy them (unless they were a prize worth taking) and kill the crew, whereas the French and Spanish – who knew the British to be better gunners, partly because their cannon had a faster trigger mechanism that improved accuracy – aimed at the rigging to try to stop the British from sailing.

At the Nile and at Copenhagen, Nelson had fought ships at anchor: Trafalgar was to be the first major battle he commanded in the open sea. Nelson's plan was to be based partly on his knowledge of the actions of a predecessor, Admiral Rodney, who had used a somewhat similar manoeuvre. He decided to abandon the dogma of line matching line and instead to split his fleet into three (subsequently two) columns and head directly for the centre and rear of the enemy line, leaving the enemy's vanguard (the ships heading the line) to sail on or attempt to turn, which could take hours, while he destroyed the other two-thirds. To succeed, he would need courage, skilled seamanship and luck: as they headed directly for the enemy line they would come under a barrage of cannonfire, but would be unable to respond as virtually all their guns could only fire sideways.

Nelson took some other steps to improve his chances: he had the ships painted 'the Nelson chequer' – black sides and gunport-lids, and a yellow stripe to mark each deck of guns. There would be no doubt whether a ship was friend or foe.

Cape Trafalgar

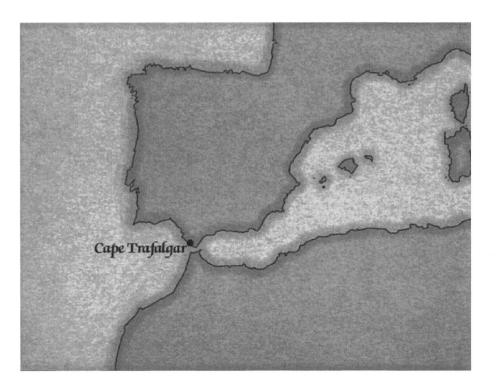

Cape Trafalgar

Nelson's flagship Victory *under sail.*

Nelson had made sure that his arrival had not been signalled by flags, so as to avoid informing the enemy of his appearance. He also withdrew the fleet out of sight of Cadiz, stationing instead only a line of small frigates to relay signals between himself and the port. The Spanish ashore could therefore see only one small frigate.

At dawn, on the 19 October, the frigate Sirius, near Cadiz, saw movement and relayed the signal back to *Victory* for which Nelson had so long been waiting: 'Enemy are coming out of port.' At 9.30 a.m. *Victory* signalled to the rest of the fleet: 'General chase, south-east.'

There was little moon the next night, and the clouds made it very dark. The combined French and Spanish fleet were still unsure of their opponent's position: Nelson had ordered that no visible lights should show on his ships. The French and Spanish, however, took no such precautions, and one British sailor wrote:

> . . . they continued to exhibit such profusions of theirs, and to make night signals in such abundance, that we seemed at times in the jaws of a mighty host ready to swallow us up.

Nelson's next concern was that Villeneuve might have second thoughts if he saw the British and return to Cadiz. His tactical sense now came into play and he ordered the British fleet to maintain a parallel course, out of sight twenty or so miles (32km) to the west. At 4 a.m. on 21 October, Nelson turned his fleet towards the north-east so that at dawn he would be less than ten miles (16km) from the enemy and a position to attack. By then, Villeneuve would be stuck between Cadiz and the Straits of Gibraltar – and committed to battle.

Nelson had an instinctive understanding of the sea. Now, in the final hours before battle, he correctly guessed that, though the day would remain relatively calm, the evening would bring a storm. Just before battle he signalled that the fleet must anchor after the engagement to save as many of the captured prizes as possible. From the moment the enemy was finally sighted, the British reckoned they had about six hours in which to prepare. During this time, Nelson wrote a final prayer in his diary:

> May the Great God, whom I worship, grant to my Country, and for the benefit of Europe in general, a great and glorious Victory; and may no misconduct in any-one tarnish it; and may humanity after Victory be the predominant feature in the British Fleet.

The long line of enemy ships, which had turned in some disarray, now stretched, crescent-shaped, in a line some four miles (6km) long. As Nelson neared, it was possible to see the different sizes. It also became apparent that Villeneuve had intermingled Spanish and French ships as he clearly did not trust the Spanish. Together, they outnumbered Nelson with thirty-three ships to his twenty-seven, with twice as many men and with 2,600 cannon to his 2,100. As the British ships were sailing with the early-morning sun behind them, the enemy had difficulty knowing just how many ships they were about to face.

Perhaps Nelson's single most important skill as a commander was his ability to inspire the disparate array of men that his ships carried. He respected his sailors and treated them with sincerity. Even though it forced Nelson into conflict with the Admiralty, he always fought for the prompt payment of wages, for improved hospital treatment and pensions, and for better provisions at sea.

> . . . [we have been brought] frocks and trowsers for the use of the Fleet under my command; but instead of their being made of good Russian duck . . . those sent are made of course wrapper-stuff, and the price increased. The issuing of such coarse stuff to the people will no doubt occasion murmur and discontent, and may have serious consequences. The contractor who furnished the stuff ought to be hanged. (*Nelson, to the Admiralty, 12 August 1804*)

Unlike so many commanders on sea and land, Nelson understood the value of keeping his men as fit as possible. He made sure his ship was regularly scrubbed, though it was impossible to remove the dank fusty smell of dry-rot, acrid bilge water, decaying stores, long-dead rats, animal manure and the men themselves, many of whom had ulcers, fever and scurvy. He also did his best to provide good supplies; indeed this aspect of his command took up an inordinate amount of time and correspondence on his part, but the healthier the ship the better a fighting vessel it became.

Nelson's long history of attention to the welfare of his crews was repaid by his men: even before Trafalgar, they loved him and would serve him to the best of their abilities. His sympathetic manner inspired his men with confidence. He was not soft, however – on the way to Cadiz he had five men flogged for theft.

Nelson displayed the same weaknesses as the ordinary seaman, who thus grew to like and respect him. Crucially, this respect was not confined to the lower decks;

his officers felt the same, considering him the 'pleasantest' superior officer they had worked with. As a result, entire crews would request that they be transferred with him whenever he changed ship.

He had trained his men well and, with battle imminent, each went to his assigned job. Furniture had been either taken into the holds or put in small boats and towed from the stern. Splinters were the most feared of all injuries – a cannonball could kill outright but a shard of wood might pierce a man like an arrow. Sand was laid on the deck to soak up the blood of battle. Muskets, guns, pistols and hand-grenades were prepared. The buckets hanging on the quarter-deck were filled with water. The surgeon and assistants prepared their meagre tools and laid them on makeshift operating tables.

Nelson also decided to send a personal message of encouragement to the fleet. He asked his signalman to hoist up the signal flags for 'England confides that every man will do his duty.' The system of flags was such that this would have taken too long as 'confides' would have needed each letter individually spelt out. Thus the signal was changed to 'England expects that every man will do his duty' and this, the most famous signal in British history, was hoisted aloft. Captain Collingwood on the *Royal Sovereign* was just one of many to wonder why Nelson sent the message: he had trained them well enough, they knew what to do.

Cannon from HMS Victory.

The ships of the Royal Navy (in blue), ranged in two columns, approach the Spanish and French fleets (in red). The furthest column was commanded by Nelson, and the nearest by Admiral Collingwood.

Having planned in meticulous detail, Nelson also knew the exact moment to launch a rapid, and often audacious, attack. The next, and final, signal made more sense to his crew: 'Close Action'. 'Close Action' had become something of a symbol for Nelson and he had used this signal before. In the past others had used it to command individual ships to get closer to an opponent but Nelson used it as a general instruction.

At this point, Nelson could do no more and the tactical command of the thirty-three ships was left to their individual captains. The commander had already won or lost the battle.

While the bands played on deck, the fleet headed straight at the enemy. One column was led by Hardy's *Victory* (with Nelson on board) and the other by Collingwood's *Royal Sovereign*. The wind, however, was not on their side – it was so light that their ships crawled along. Until they could reach the enemy they would be sitting targets. Both the *Victory* and *Royal Sovereign* might have to withstand up to an hour of cannon fire from five or six ships each before they could respond – and it was the Franco-Spanish intention to sink every British ship before the British could even fire back.

Nelson paced the deck, expecting a 'warm' afternoon. The first enemy shot, fired at extreme range, flew overhead. Another shot punched through a main sail. A further shot narrowly missed Nelson but hit his secretary standing nearby. The man was killed instantly and thrown overboard. Then a shot smashed the ship's wheel, necessitating the assignment of forty seamen to manipulate the huge tiller with ropes.

Initially, to keep the enemy guessing, *Victory* had been steering for the enemy's leading ships but now they altered course towards the centre – towards the twelfth in the line. They were looking for Villeneuve's flagship, hoping to fight her, ship to ship. As Villeneuve's flag could not be seen, *Victory* headed for the biggest ship, the *Santissima Trinidad* (four decks and 140 guns), which they thought would probably have one of the two admirals on board. Behind her was the French 80-gun *Bucentaure* and the 74-gun *Redoubtable*; by chance, Villeneuve was, in fact, on board the *Bucentaure*. Soon after noon, *Victory* was within a short distance of the enemy, who had failed in their desperate attempts to stop the British approach. Captain Hardy asked him which of the three nearest ships, all firing into *Victory,* they should attack first. Nelson replied that it did not matter.

Oil sketch of Horatio Nelson by John Hoppner

When Villeneuve's *Bucentaure* had joined battle with the *Victory*, he had signalled to Rear-Admiral Dumanoir, who commanded the leading ships, to turn back and support him. But the wind was so light (and it was suggested afterwards that his motivation equally so) that of the ten ships which managed to turn, only five joined the fighting, and those not until too late in the battle.

Victory was now only 100 feet (30m) from *Bucentaure*. Soon she could fire her first broadside of fifty cannon. The men on the tiller strained to keep the ship headed straight, very close to *Bucentaure's* stern windows. It was almost within touching distance and the French flag lapped *Victory's* bow. Suddenly, through the gunports, the gunners could see the enemy and they unleashed a furious volley of shot: cast-shot, grape-shot, chain-shot and bar-shot – each designed to kill men, smash wood or destroy masts and rigging. *Victory's* gunners could not see the effect of their first discharge through the wood dust and smoke but they could hear the screams of the dying and wounded. The gunners themselves were quickly deafened and blood dripped from punctured eardrums and noses. The confusion of battle was accentuated by the almost continuous invisibility of both friend and foe. Hardy then steered for *Redoubtable* and within minutes it too was under fire from *Victory's* starboard guns.

On board *Victory*, Nelson could only watch as the battle raged. Royal Marine Second Lieutenant Rotely, on *Victory*, recalled:

> We were engaging on both sides; every gun was going off. . . . recoiling with
> violence, reports louder than thunder, the decks heaving and the sides straining.
> I fancied myself in the infernal regions, where every man appeared a devil. Lips
> might move, but orders and hearing were out of the question; everything was
> done by signs.

Victory carried on fighting *Redoubtable* on her starboard and then engaged the massive *Santissima Trinidad* on her port side. *Victory* was right alongside *Redoubtable* whereas *Santissima Trinidad* was a little further away. As fate would have it, Captain Lucas of the *Redoubtable* was one of the few captains who had used the time in Cadiz wisely. His crew had not been able to practise firing cannon while moored in port – as the British had been able to at sea – so he had instructed his men in boarding and close-arms fire. Chance had brought him alongside *Victory* and he hoped to put into effect all these hours of instruction. He ordered his men to board. First, grappling hooks were thrown on board *Victory* and then, to British amazement, *Redoubtable* stopped firing and all its gunports shut so that British boarders could not climb in. Lucas then brought up his marines in preparation to board, while sharpshooters stationed in the rigging were attempting to clear *Victory's* upper decks.

Nelson had rejected any suggestion that he should not wear his distinctive vice-admiral's uniform and medals during the battle. He wanted his sailors to see him and know he was exposed to the same dangers as they were. It made him an easy target,

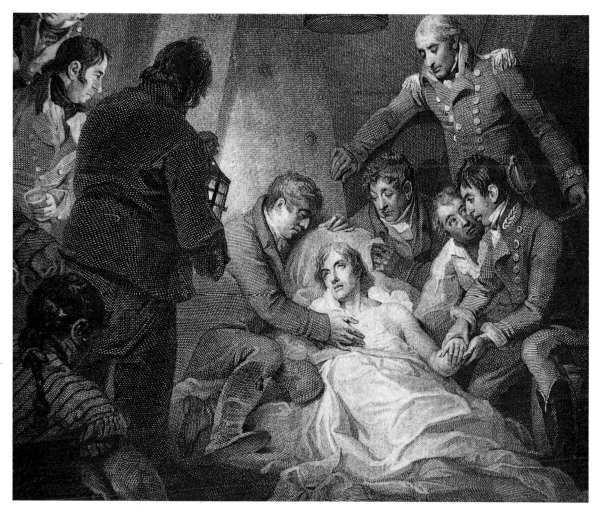

The Death of Nelson, after the painting by Devis.

of course, with Lucas' snipers only tens of feet (5–6m) away and aiming straight at him. But he refused to take cover, though he ordered others to do so – a mixture of courage, preoccupation and faith. At 1.15 p.m., when only a handful of the sharp-shooters remained, the rest having been shot away by the British marines and cannon, a musket ball hit Nelson in the shoulder, passed through a lung and lodged in his spine. He fell to the deck, murmuring: 'They have done for me at last, Hardy, my backbone is shot through.'

Lucas, having cleared *Victory's* decks, sensed success and had 200 marines ready to board. At that very moment, however, the British ship *Temeraire* appeared through the smoke, crashed into *Redoubtable* and unleashed a furious broadside that killed most of the 200 marines. The battle carried on and *Victory* continued to fire, despite being very severely damaged. Villenueve's ship, the *Bucentaure*, had also been wrecked, first by *Victory*, then by *Conqueror*, and she was now stranded, with only one of her three masts still standing. When that last mast was shot down

*The Battle of Trafalgar,
by Luny.*

Villeneuve could play no further part: he could send no more signals to his fleet and thus no action could be taken as a result of any command. At 2.15 p.m. he surrendered his flagship to the *Conqueror* and was taken prisoner.

The action was now a succession of duels between individual ships, firing broadsides into each other at point-blank range. The superiority of British guns and crews assured success. Spasmodically, news reached *Victory* of one French or Spanish ship after another surrendering.

Hardy was busy in the fight, but when he could he went down to see Nelson and congratulated him on a 'brilliant victory'. It was complete, he said, and though he did not know how many enemy ships had surrendered, he was certain of having taken fourteen or fifteen. The British had lost no ships, but nearly 1,700 men had been killed or wounded. The Franco-Spanish fleet had suffered 6,000 casualties, including Gravina; eighteen ships were captured or destroyed in action, and 20,000 men, including Admiral Villeneuve, taken prisoner.

Some of the many British sailors wounded at Trafalgar died before they could be transported back to Britain, and were buried in Gibraltar.

Lieutenant
WILLIAM FORSTER
Late of
His Majesty, Ship Colofsus
Died of the Wounds
He Recieved in the
Glorious Battle off Trafalgar
the 21 Day of Octr 1805
Aged 20 Years.

It was a great success, but to the crew this was far overshadowed by a greater tragedy: at 4.30 p.m. Nelson died.

Although the success of Trafalgar effectively secured a century of British domination over the seas, at the time the death of Nelson darkened any victory. There was widespread public grief, culminating in an elaborate, emotional funeral in St Paul's Cathedral. Nelson had left a profound impression on the nation's psyche and had become a model for a new breed of middle-class professional officer prepared to commit his life to king and country. Nelson's career showed that the aristocracy was not the only source of good leaders. His relatively humble roots and varied early years of service had created in Nelson an affinity with the ordinary sailor which bridged the gap between commander and commanded. He understood tactics and would brave any danger but, at sea, all that would have been as nothing had not his men – from officer to servant boy – been willing to give all for their Lord Nelson. A Lieutenant Ellis commented that his men were disconcerted to receive the famous signal at Trafalgar and murmured:

> "Do our duty! Of course we'll do our duty! Let us come alongside of 'em, and we'll soon show whether we'll do our duty." Still, the men cheered vociferously – more I believe from love and admiration of their Admiral and leader than from a full appreciation of this well-known signal.

Time after time, Nelson led his men into battle and was never known to flinch from the possibility of injury or death. Even at Trafalgar, with snipers close by, he stood his ground. He acted with the certainty of one assured of justice and success, a courage partly born of the faith he inherited from his father. As a child in Burnham Thorpe, Nelson was much affected by his father's church. In a sense, he saw himself as a Christian warrior, fighting off the 'fiery assaults' of England's enemies. Of course, he felt fear – and, at times, great pain – but he overcame these and earned the respect of all around him. Like Alexander the Great, Nelson's scars meant little more to him than records of the battles he had fought. Despite his diminished sight, the loss of an arm, his concussion at the Nile, his continued sea-sickness, and increasing exhaustion ('I am grown old and battered to pieces'), he carried on, not for money or power but patriotism and honour: 'True honour, I hope, predominates in my mind far above riches.'

For almost a century, Trafalgar was studied in great detail and its lessons provided much instruction to the captains of the empire, for Nelson had been willing to risk his life for 'the greater good'. He believed that 'Life with disgrace is dreadful. A glorious death is to be envied.' Fortunate perhaps to have survived as long as he did, his luck ran out at Trafalgar but he died what for many was a glorious death. He had probably intended to retire after this final campaign and live with Emma in Sicily, but instead he was killed at the moment of his greatest victory, a poignant conclusion to a life of brilliant, selfless and courageous leadership.

CHAPTER FOUR

NAPOLEON BONAPARTE

'What are the lives of a million men to a man such as I?' (Napoleon)

For nearly twenty years Napoleon Bonaparte led the armies of France to victory. The great powers of Russia, Prussia and Austria, as well as numerous smaller states and principalities, buckled time and again beneath the weight of his abilities. He had personal qualities and military prowess beyond equal, supported by administrative, social and military systems that he created himself.

Napoleon's great assets were his mathematical mind, phenomenal memory, boundless energy and prolific imagination. He studied enemy personalities, terrains, supplies and manoeuvres, and would consider all eventualities before acting. Even today, his writings and maxims are pored over in military academies throughout the world.

He sought immortality through conquest and feared nothing worse than the passing of time: 'space we can recover, time never'. The Battle of Austerlitz, the culmination of a stunning campaign, demonstrates just why Napoleon valued time so highly.

The island of Corsica had only been part of France for a year when, on 15 August 1769, Napoleon Buonaparte was born. He was one of thirteen children of whom only eight survived infancy. Its position in the Mediterranean made Corsica a valuable prize and so its possession had changed hands on a number of occasions. This great 'Frenchman' could just as easily have been born British.

Aged nine, the Italian-speaking Napoleon and his elder brother Joseph were sent to Autun in France to learn French. They went on to Brienne, a school run along military lines for the sons of relatively wealthy parents. Napoleon was small, quietly spoken and homesick and soon found himself being bullied for his Corsican accent, acquiring the nickname 'straw-nose'. Reacting to such hostility, Napoleon showed a precocious ability for organizing elaborate war-games. This, and an aptitude for mathematics and science, eventually earned him the respect of his peers and teachers.

Napoleon at his command post. Detail of the Battle of Austerlitz, by Gérard.

Napoleon in 1785, aged sixteen, from the earliest known sketch from life. It was drawn during the year he spent at the Ecole Militaire in Paris.

In 1784, he entered the military academy in Paris. During the first year, his father died and the school allowed him to pass out a year early so that he could seek employment to support his family. Napoleon joined an artillery regiment at Valence, this being one of the few military options open to him. The cavalry and infantry were the province of the higher aristocracy. Such pompous attitudes only fuelled the young Napoleon's ambitions.

In June 1788, he was posted to Auxonne, a small garrison town in Burgundy. His commanding officer encouraged the young Bonaparte to read the works of the brilliant military tactician le Comte de Guibert. His views were that the successful commander should achieve numerical superiority at a key point, launch an all-out attack at this point and exploit the element of surprise by swiftness of movement. These were the very ideas later incorporated into so-called Napoleonic strategy. Napoleon was never to be an original thinker; his strength lay in the acquisition and exploitation of knowledge.

Napoleon was growing up in a France undergoing radical and violent change. The privileged aristocracy he resented were about to be crushed, and the Bourbon monarchy and the old regime swept away. During the ensuing French Revolution the military did not stand by its king, Louis XVI, preferring instead to await the outcome. Napoleon, for his part, though he believed political change was inevitable, was little involved, preferring to spend his time studying the art of gunnery. His brothers, however, foresaw that Napoleon had long-term ambitions: 'I can tell you in complete confidence', Lucien wrote to Joseph, 'that I have always discerned in Napoleon a purely personal ambition, which overrules his patriotism . . . . He seems to me to have a strong leaning towards tyranny.'

Several French towns resisted the Republic and one of these was the southern port and arsenal of Toulon. This action was a stroke of luck for the young artillery gunner (who had changed his name to the French spelling, Bonaparte). The siege of Toulon from 7 September to 19 December 1793, was the moment Napoleon, aged twenty-four, came to both public and official notice. The Republic was weakened by factional in-fighting and rebellion. Those who had lost power in the revolution saw this as their opportunity to take it back. On 28 August, Toulon, having sided with the cause of the young King Louis XVII, admitted the British fleet under Admiral Lord Hood into their port. At a stroke, France's naval power in the Mediterranean was threatened.

Bonaparte at Auxonne, 1788, by Francois Flameng. The year Napoleon spent at the Auxonne Artillery School laid the foundations of his outstanding military career.

A force was immediately sent to retake Toulon. The artillery commander who was to lead the guns was wounded and Napoleon brashly presented himself as the ideal replacement. In an effort to associate himself with the winning side, Napoleon had recently written a political pamphlet which argued that the ideals of the revolution must be supported. Benefiting from the favourable reception his pamphlet had received and from family connections, he was appointed to the vacancy.

On arrival at Toulon, Napoleon immediately isolated the key to the siege and assessed how to position his artillery. After a great deal of resistance from his superiors he was allowed to follow his instincts. Displaying an early understanding of the military mind, he dubbed his exposed and dangerous position the 'Batterie des hommes san peur' – 'the battery of men without fear'. He had no problem recruiting soldiers to serve there.

As a result of his bombardment and a subsequent 7,000-man attack, in which Napoleon was bayonetted in the thigh, the key fort was captured. The British fleet fled. All agreed that the young commander deserved most of the credit, and he was *The Storming of the* promoted to 'general de brigade' (brigadier-general). Augustin de Robespierre, a *Bastille, 14 July 1789, by* political commissar with the army, wrote to his brother Maximilien, by then de facto *J-B Lallemand, Museé* ruler of France, praising the 'transcendant merit' of the young officer.
Carnavalet, Paris.

Execution of Louis XVI, 21 January 1793, Musée Carnavalet, Paris.

The political situation in Paris was highly volatile and when the government was overthrown, Napoleon was temporarily jailed for his connections with Robespierre. He was released after a few weeks and, although the new government feared his ambition, they valued his ability and offered him various positions. These, however, he turned down as being too inconsequential.

In October 1795, royalist unrest gave Napoleon's career another boost. A crowd had marched on the government, which was unsure if the commander of the Army of the Interior would, if necessary, open fire to maintain order. Just in case he refused, they installed Napoleon as his second-in-command – they felt sure that he would not suffer any such moral doubts. They were right: declaring that a 'whiff of grapeshot' would solve the problem, he killed 200 demonstrators with his artillery. The regime had been saved. Napoleon was rewarded with the command of the Army of the Interior and made military adviser to the government. A few months later, on 2 March 1796, he was placed in charge of the Army of Italy.

Italy was at this time effectively an Austrian province and Napoleon had submitted a plan for its conquest and absorbtion in to France. Now he had his chance to prove that his plan would work.

When he first arrived at Nice he found not the troops he had expected, but fewer than 40,000 demoralized, ill-equipped and ill-treated men. But, unbowed, he began to work to transform this ragged, hungry and dispirited body of men into a victorious army. As British General Wavell later wrote:

Bust of Napoleon aged thirty, by Corbet, Musée Carnavalet, Paris.

If you can discover how a young, unknown man inspired a ragged, mutinous, half-starved army, and made it fight; how he gave it energy and momentum to march and fight as it did; how he dominated and controlled generals older and more experienced than himself – then you will have learnt something. Napoleon did not gain so much by a study of rules and strategy, as by a profound knowledge of human nature in war.

Napoleon addressed his men:

Soldiers, you are naked, badly fed . . . . Rich provinces and great towns will be in your power, and in them you will find honour, glory, wealth. Soldiers of Italy, will you be wanting in courage and steadfastness?

He told his troops that if they captured the enemy's stores, all their problems would be solved. His inspirational rhetoric rallied his troops, but was not enough to convince his army's veteran generals. However, using the knowledge acquired from his years of study, Napoleon soon captivated them too with his fresh, dynamic approach to strategic and tactical manoeuvres. One general had to admit that, despite himself, 'this little devil of a general inspired me with awe'.

Between April 1796 and April 1797, Napoleon performed a brilliant series of strategic moves that allowed him to divide and defeat his enemies. In this campaign he faced every kind of military action. By adapting his inferior military resources to meet changing challenges, he first defeated the Austrians at Montenotte on 12 April 1796 and then the Piedmontese at Mondovi on 21 April. He defeated the Austrians again at Lodi on 10 May. In that battle Napoleon personally sighted the guns along a river bank, earning himself the nickname 'the little corporal' (as corporals were supposed to site guns). He captured Milan on 21 May. Thereafter the need to besiege the powerful Austrian fortress of Mantua entailed the defeat of three Austrian attempts to raise the siege. In January 1797, with northern Italy under French control, Napoleon invaded Austria. By 6 April he was within sight of Vienna and the Austrian emperor sued for an armistice, which led to peace.

Back in France the political hierarchy was under constant threat from royalists and needed Napoleon's support. Having gained the first real victory for France in five years of European war, his popularity among the general public had reached new peaks. Napoleon left Italy where he had been doing more or less as he pleased, and returned to France. He was sent to the Atlantic coast to command the planned invasion of England but he concluded that the idea was ludicrous until France had command of the seas. It would be much cleverer, he said, to strike Britain where it would hurt most – at its trade. If he could occupy Turkish-controlled Egypt, he would break one of Britain's important trade routes to India. The economic effects might force Britain to make peace.

The French government were happy to approve his plan and he was assigned an army of 40,000 troops. The next problem was how to get to Egypt: the Royal Navy might well catch them. Napoleon set sail in the knowledge that if he was spotted by the British fleet he would almost certainly be attacked and sunk. As luck would have it, his fleet evaded an engagement, though on two occasions they came perilously close to being seen.

Napoleon won two battles; the first at Alexandria, the second at the Battle of the Pyramids. Disaster, however, struck the French fleet when Nelson destroyed the French navy at the Battle of the Nile. Napoleon's mobility was effectively destroyed, and his dangerous lines of supply and retreat to France, broken.

Nevertheless, he stayed and proceeded to introduce new political institutions, administration and technical skills to Egypt. Like Alexander, Napoleon brought with him builders, administrators, naturalists and so on. He even brought a composer and a balloonist. In total he had with him 500 'savants' (wise men) with which he aimed not only to conquer but to incorporate his conquests into an expanding area of French influence. But his plans did not go smoothly and Turkey, who considered Egypt its own, declared war. In response, Napoleon marched north to confront them. He only got as far as Acre when plague and news of an impending seaborne Turkish invasion of Egypt forced him to retreat. Only a third of his army survived and these he soon abandoned to their fate. He had had enough: he boarded a small ship and, again evading British capture, sailed back to France.

If ever a country was ripe for dictatorship, that country was France in 1799. People on the streets of Paris were calling for military rule to restore order and pride. The old government collapsed under the weight of its own corruption and inefficiency and, on 9-10 November 1799, there was a coup. With two leading politicians, Napoleon took power. These three 'consuls' – a term appropriated from Roman history – promised a return to glory.

His accomplices saw Napoleon as a way of assuring military support, but they underestimated his political abilities. He soon ousted them and became First Consul. Although the French did not want the return of a monarch, they did want a strong, charismatic leader. Napoleon was expected to secure a lasting peace, an end to disorder and, as a man of the Revolution himself, consolidate the social and political advances promised in the Declaration of the Rights of Man.

Yet he was also a slave to ambition. Like Julius Caesar, he thought of himself before all else. He did not believe in the pre-eminence of the 'people': he mocked the ease with which he could control them with gestures and display. But, he was also in many ways an enlightened leader. It was a military dictatorship, but the nature of a political system is often irrelevant in comparison to the way in which power is wielded.

The Constitution of 1799 placed complete power in Napoleon's hands – he alone could appoint generals, ministers, civil servants and magistrates. Using this power he

The Emperor Napoleon wearing his favourite uniform – colonel of the Chasseurs de la Garde, a cavalry regiment of the Imperial Guard – by Lefevre, Musée Carnavalet, Paris.

began to change profoundly all the major institutions of France. He reformed the judicial system and ended the corrupt election of judges. Chaos in French commerce was reordered: he created the Banque de France and altered financial and taxation policies. Education became a public service and universities were reopened. Napoleon offered hope to the poor and work (not least in the army), and to the bourgeoisie he proclaimed the values of authority, property and the family. The bravest measure he took was to reverse the Republic's decision to outlaw religion: 'How are we to create social customs? There is only one way and that is to re-establish religion.'

In his view the people of France preferred glory to liberty. They were sick of internal fratricide and appearing to be the weak man of Europe. They were embarrassed by naval defeats and Britain's colonial superiority. Napoleon believed that they sought a leader to give them hope and ambition again. For a time, he maintained the title of Republic and showed respect for the outward signs of revolution but at the Tuileries Gardens he erected statues of autocrats like Alexander and Caesar, upon whom he modelled himself.

Naturally, Napoleon relied upon the skills and resources of his soldiers. The old army had belonged to the king rather than the French nation. It had been slowly improving before the Revolution but it always lacked a proper recruiting system and took whoever it could by persuasion, fraud or force, often filling its ranks with criminals, deserters and foreigners. The gulf between officers and men had become an

The volunteer's leave-taking, Musée Carnavalet, Paris. Although many Frenchmen joined up willingly in the early stages of France's revolutionary wars, Napoleon's military successes depended on his ability to raise huge armies of conscripts.

abyss, the chances of promotion based on talent grew thinner every year. Before the Revolution, there was little national spirit or patriotism within the army. The king, Louis XVI, should have been at its centre, its motivating force, but he had proved incapable of maintaining or leading it. A man like Napoleon, therefore, came as welcome relief as he dedicated great efforts towards his army.

The Revolution had created a nation-at-arms. Fighting was no longer the duty of a small body of men or even citizen militia – the entire country was now involved.

> . . . all Frenchmen are permanently requisitioned for service into the armies. Young men will go forth to battle; married men will forge weapons and transport munitions; women will make tents and clothing and serve in hospitals; children will make lint from old linen; and old men will be brought to the public squares to arouse the courage of the soldiers, while preaching the unity of the Republic and hatred against Kings.
> (*Revolutionary declaration*)

Such armies followed the flags and slogans of the Revolution. Napoleon used this to his own ends and slowly replaced revolutionary fervour with enthusiasm for his own person and prepared these same soldiers to travel beyond France's borders, living off the land as they went. He continued to insist on conscription. Men recruited at these annual call-ups were sent to regimental depots for basic training before being sent to regiments in the field. The more casualties Napoleon suffered in a year, the more men were called up the following year.

In early 1800, Napoleon prepared to attack Austria. As a fighting man, Napoleon always wished to be at the head of his army. As Consul, however, the Constitution did not allow him to command and he therefore gave nominal authority to his chief of staff, Berthier. As spring approached, he began his attack, first moving with daring and speed across the Alpine Great St Bernard Pass. Napoleon loved to be seen suffering, as great commanders had before him. Quoting Caesar, he declared that it was better to die gloriously than live defeated. He also commissioned the artist David to paint him on a rearing white charger, pointing the way across the Alps. In reality he crossed on a mule, led by a guide, falling off twice.

The attack on Austria was two-pronged. First some troops were sent along the Danube; Napoleon then crossed the Alps and caught the Austrians by surprise. They had never imagined he would attempt to cross the mountains while the snow still lay on the ground. Nevertheless, the subsequent Battle of Marengo on 14 June was bitterly fought and only won by the French due to the timely arrival of Desaix, one of Napoleon's generals. Peace was agreed in February 1801.

Only Britain remained at war with France, but both countries were exhausted and signed a peace treaty at Amiens in March 1802. Napoleon now felt more than entitled to ask for – and was subsequently awarded – the title of First Consul for life. He had brought peace as he had promised. He was not, however, universally popular – and murder plots, backed by monarchists, rival political groups or foreign interests such as Britain, were launched, unsuccessfully, against him.

Napoleon believed that between monarchies and a young republic a spirit of hostility must always exist. 'Every peace treaty means no more than a brief armistice.' He used the breathing space offered by the Treaty of Amiens to perfect his weapon – his Grande Armée.

Unlike the localized battles of previous centuries, Napoleonic warfare was a large and sprawling affair, fought simultaneously on several fronts. Napoleon could personally monitor a vital spot but had to rely on his newly created Marshals of the Empire, such as Ney, Lannes and Davout. These young men were told what to do and when to do it, but the details of the fighting were left up to them. They in turn had to rely on their divisional commanders. In such conditions a commander needed trustworthy men to act as his eyes and ears.

By 1805, Napoleon had an Imperial Headquarters of 400 officers, divided between his personal HQ (the Emperor's Cabinet, which was the key nerve centre, the map office, the Emperor's Household, the tactical HQ run by Berthier), the General HQ

Napoleon at work in the Emperor's cabinet. His grasp of the details of military and state affairs allowed him to dictate simultaneously any number of orders and letters.

(also run by Berthier) and the Administrative HQ (behind the lines, specializing in logistics).

The Grande Armée (numbering about 500,000 men) was organized into self-contained corps d'armée. Each corps had its own staff and comprised varying numbers of infantry divisions, a light cavalry brigade or division, and a heavy artillery detachment under corps command. There were also bridging and engineer detachments, supply and medical units.

The size of each corps depended on its intended role and Napoleon's opinion of its commander; it could vary from 10,000 to 40,000. These corps were, in effect, miniature armies, which were always within supporting range (a day's march: 20-25 miles) of one another.

It is not surprising, given his military background, that Napoleon had great belief in the power of artillery, if fire was concentrated against a single point. 'It is with guns that war is made,' he declared. He knew the enemy had better cavalry but realized that artillery would soon all but rule the battlefield. Small units of men with artillery could pin down an entire army. Topography was now much more important and a campaign could be won with the compass as much as with a charge. Indeed, cavalry charges were all but obsolete in the face of massed artillery. Napoleon was thus fortunate that the French artillery was the best in Europe – a product of lighter barrels, excellent casting methods and well-trained crews.

Napoleon drove his officers to their physical limits. He had a special coach made to suit his needs. A partitioned seat across the rear allowed two people to work without disturbing one another. The coach contained maps, a writing desk, writing materials, a travelling library, clothes and toilet articles, food and drink. One of Napoleon's specially designed camp beds was stowed under the coachman's seat.

Once at the battlefield Napoleon mounted one of his horses, which had been specially trained to be docile and suit a small man. He had learnt to ride as a boy in Corsica and had undergone further training at the Royal Military School in Paris, but was not a natural, or indeed a good, rider. He was short and ungainly and often seemed to have his mind on other matters. Yet he rode further and longer than most monarchs or generals of his generation. He had a number of falls, some of them serious. In twenty years of campaigning he had several horses shot from under him. Like other great commanders, he had his share of good fortune. When discussing the qualities of other generals and officers he would often ask, 'Yes, but is he lucky?'

The campaign of 1805 that culminated in the Battle of Austerlitz demonstrates three of Napoleon's most important qualities: his strategic skills, his carefully cultivated relationship with his soldiers and his tactical ability.

The British had become increasingly unhappy at Napoleon's virtual control of the entire European coastline from Italy to Belgium. Relations were further worsened when Britain refused (as the Treaty of Amiens had stipulated) to return Malta to the French. War resumed in May 1803.

Napoleon dressed in his coronation robes, by Ingres, Musée de L'Armée, Paris. The coronation was planned for maximum theatrical effect. At the most solemn moment, Napoleon took the crown from the hands of the Pope, who had been coerced into attending and, symbolically rejecting any higher authority, crowned himself Emperor.

It was initially a slow-moving, essentially naval conflict, with neither participant in any position to fully commit. Britain needed support from her European allies but these were too weak or unwilling to help. On 14 March 1804, Napoleon ordered the capture and execution of the French prince, the Duc d'Enghien. This, it was claimed, was in response to a British-funded plot, encouraged by the monarchist court-in-exile in London, to assassinate Napoleon. As the prince was related to monarchs throughout Europe, peace was doomed. Britain initiated a new coalition with Austria (250,000 troops), Russia (200,000 troops), Sweden and Naples. The aim was that the British fleet and her allies' armies would cut Napoleon down to size by reducing France to its original pre-Revolution frontiers.

Napoleon felt himself more than a match for these foreign opponents. He concerned himself with the reconstruction of France and devoted much of his time to working on new laws and decrees. He also furthered his own grip on power. On 2 December 1804, in an hugely elaborate ceremony, he crowned himself emperor. Eventually, members of his family were made princes and princesses, kings and queens. An imperial nobility was created.

He continued to reform the administration and progressively introduced the Code Napoleon – which embraced new civil, commercial and judicial legislation. For a short while these developments at home and the relative calm in Europe brought satisfaction to the French people, despite severe restrictions on internal dissent. However, Napoleon knew that this calm was illusory and saw that full-scale war was just around the corner.

His plans to invade Britain were, however, crumbling about him. The Battle of Trafalgar (21 October 1805) would be the final confirmation that he had no chance of defeating Britain while its navy remained so formidable.

Indeed, long before Trafalgar, Napoleon had seen that his invasion plans were going to fail and, on 25 August, he ordered most of his 200,000 strong army to break camp at Boulogne and march east. However, he stayed on the coast until 3 September to appear as if he still intended to invade Britain. While he was there, he examined different strategic possibilities and ordered officers and spies to provide detailed reports on, for example, the topography of the land across which he, or the enemy, might move. Napoleon wrote to Berthier in early September requesting:

> . . . somebody who is acquainted with German to follow the march of the Austrian regiments, and file the details in the compartments of the box you were told to make for that purpose. The name and number of each regiment is to be entered on a playing card, and the cards are to be changed from one compartment to another according to the movements of the regiments.

Having weighed up all the possibilities, Napoleon decided to leave 30,000 men near the Channel in case the British tried to land, send some 50,000 men to northern Italy to act as a distraction, and take the bulk of the army (210,000) from the Rhine to the Danube. He intended to beat the Austrians before the Russians, currently en route, could arrive to help their allies. The Prussians, who would be formidable opponents if they added their 200,000 troops to the campaign, were still dithering about whether to join the coalition. Napoleon offered them Hanover as a bribe to stay out of the way.

The Austrians had three armies prepared – 94,000 in northern Italy, 72,000 on the Danube and 22,000 in the Tyrolean Alpine passes. The Russian force of 100,000 were supposed to arrive and launch an attack across the Rhine into central France. But Napoleon calculated that the Austrians were vulnerable while they were waiting for their allies.

By 10 September the allies were still slumbering. Only the Austrian General Mack had achieved anything by occupying Bavaria (one of Napoleon's few allies) and the strategically important city of Ulm, on the River Danube. There he awaited the promised Russian support, unaware that the Russians were using a different calendar, twelve days behind. The Russians under their commander Kutusov, a skilled veteran, were therefore still some way distant.

Napoleon knew that his enemies could both outnumber and outflank him but were dependent on slow baggage trains and communications. His best chance therefore lay with speed and surprise. He swept in his men from many parts of the French Empire to face the opposition.

Napoleon's rapid strategic offensive was intended to parry the Austrians in the Tyrol and Italy, defeat Mack, then hit the Russians before occupying Vienna. Five corps of men and Napoleon's own Imperial Guard and Reserve Cavalry – a force of 210,000 men with 400 cannon – were to 'march dispersed, fight concentrated'.

The first conflict was against Mack while he waited at the Danube. Napoleon ordered troops from Hanover, Boulogne and Utrecht towards Ulm. Although he tried not to overmarch them to the point of total exhaustion, he still pushed his troops to cover 20-25 miles a day. Napoleon wanted, as always, a short, sharp campaign in which he would exert the maximum effort over a short period. Despite the fact that it was autumn and the stored harvests were easy for Napoleon's troops to steal, he did not have the supplies to survive a long campaign.

It took the troops only eleven days to march from the Rhine to within striking distance of Mack, who suddenly realized he was about to be attacked from the rear. French troops had been cleverly diverting Mack's attention by continual forward and backward moves from the direction of the Black Forest and the Austrians seemed paralysed when they found the attack coming from the opposite direction. After a number of skirmishes between 7 and 20 October, they surrendered. By the end of October, at the cost of only 2,000 men, Napoleon had captured 60,000 men and 200 cannon. It was an almost perfect strategic victory.

The Russians were shocked and hastily retreated as Napoleon chased them along the Danube. Kutusov felt it was vital that they regroup with the remaining Austrians and other Russian troops, north of Vienna. The chase was fierce but Kutusov successfully escaped.

On 15 November, the French entered Vienna, where they appropriated a huge arsenal of 100,000 muskets, 2,000 cannon and vast stores of ammunition. Using a bridge across the Danube, which one of Napoleon's officers had captured by pretending that an armistice had been signed, he continued in pursuit of Kutusov. Napoleon arrived in Znaim on the 17 October and decided that his exhausted army would soon have to rest and resupply. By now he had only 53,000 troops; the rest had been lost en route to sickness, injury or desertion, or had been left behind to guard the supply lines.

The Austro-Russians numbered over 80,000 and more were marching up from the south. Napoleon had to take a calculated risk. He could not wait: at any moment the extra Austrian reinforcements might arrive or Prussia might enter the war to take advantage of his apparent weakness. Napoleon was indeed stretched to his limits, though not as weak as he wanted his enemy to believe, and now was the time to find the site on which to draw out the battle.

One of Napoleon's greatest skills was his ability to understand and use geography to his advantage. Near the town of Austerlitz, he saw the terrain on which he decided to fight what he hoped would be a decisive battle. On 21 November he carefully inspected the countryside, walking over an area of small hills and streams. He ordered that the front side of one of the hills, the Santon Feature where his left wing

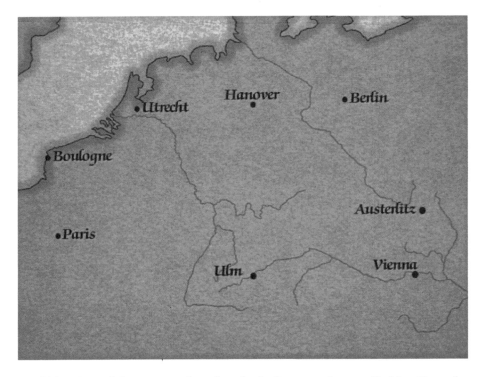

The northern European arena, across which unfolded the campaign which culminated in the decisive Battle of Austerlitz.

would be situated, be excavated so that the incline was sharper. To his officers he declared: 'Gentlemen, examine this ground carefully. It is going to be a battlefield.'

The key to his plan was to lure the Austro-Russians into a trap. To do this he ordered a small group of troops to occupy Austerlitz and the nearby Pratzen Heights. He hoped that his small army would be too tempting for the enemy, about thirty miles (48km) away, to resist. Meanwhile he intended to force-march his I and III Corps from Iglau and Vienna to increase his numbers to 75,000. His soldiers commented wryly: 'Our Emperor makes war not with our arms but with our legs.'

The Russians and Austrians were having a difficult time cooperating. Some resentment was still felt for the Russian non-appearance at Ulm, and the Russians, for their part, were scornful of the Austrian defeat. Bitter rivalries fermented between officers. Both Napoleon and the Austro-Russians sent envoys to talk about an armistice: the French in order to appear vulnerable, the Austro-Russians to play for time while their reinforcements came up from the south. Napoleon was not fooled and while the talks went on, he continued to bring up and deploy his reinforcements, using cavalry movements to disguise his actions. The Allies, however, became increasingly convinced that the French army was as good as beaten.

Napoleon then made his next move: he told his surprised subordinates on the forward line to make a 'panic' retreat from Austerlitz and the dominating Pratzen Heights. In effect, he handed over the best ground to the enemy who, as Napoleon intended, saw such actions as those of a desperate army. In some disorder, the Austro-Russian forces made their way forward to take over these important positions. Meanwhile, Napoleon's reinforcements, some of whom had marched sixty-four miles (103km) in forty-eight hours, had all arrived by the evening of 1 December.

Napoleon knew the value of being close to his soldiers: 'a general's principle talent consists in knowing the mentality of the soldier and gaining his confidence'. He had the power of personality to create a feeling of devotion equalled only by a few other great commanders. He also understood the value of such loyalty and was cynical of how easily his troops could be directed; on one occasion while handing out a new issue of medals he remarked 'with such baubles, men are led'.

Napoleon understood the strengths and weaknesses of the French soldier, which varied from courage in success to disproportionate dejection after failure. He continually used psychological methods, presenting unit colours, awarding battle honours, giving rewards, presenting medals, bestowing titles, or hurling merciless castigation and contempt at those who failed him. His very presence often inspired valour in the youngest conscript or most battle-worn veteran.

> Although the campaign had only lasted two months we were barefooted . . . worn out with fatigue, wet through with rain and snow, nipped with cold, and camped in the mud . . . . The Emperor knew of our wants and our fatigue, which he shared. He was aware, too, that the soldiers grumbled . . . and he said, 'They are right; but it is to spare their blood that I make them undergo these hardships.' When we heard that, he could have made us do what no one else could. (*Captain Charles François*)

The site of the battle of Austerlitz at dawn.

Napoleon projected a careful mix of the grand and the common. He used every means of propaganda – the press, war bulletins, the pageantry of a noble empire, the artful creation of his own legend – and would lie as frequently as he thought necessary to ensure success. He tried to be a soldier among soldiers, a father among his children. He could talk to them, collectively or man-to-man, in their own terms (not excluding a few popular expletives) and was an expert at soldier's slang. It was crucial to his image that he be perceived as a general who shared their perils and discomforts.

Nevertheless, there had been mass looting at Ulm, followed by a long march and Napoleon knew that he had to restore both the discipline and morale of his troops before the battle. On the evening of 1 December he presented himself to his men.

The Battle of Austerlitz, after the painting by Gerard. General Rapp presents prisoners of the Russian Chevalier Garde to the Emperor.

Although a group of marshals and officers clothed in the finest suits of military regalia rode behind him, the Emperor himself wore a threadbare, undistinguished uniform. He walked among the camp fires and soon a torchlight procession was formed to mark the first anniversary of his coronation as emperor. Napoleon claimed this was the best evening of his life.

Having ensured the enthusiasm of his soldiers, Napoleon now turned to tactical matters. Having slept for only a few hours, he awoke at 3 a.m. his mind, as ever, juggling facts and figures, possibilities and plans. He issued orders to strengthen the French right wing. At 4 a.m. the first trumpets and bugles were sounded. On both sides of the Goldbach Stream, which marked the boundary between the rival armies, opposing formations began to take shape. The valley and the Pratzen Heights were

Overview of the battlesite of Austerlitz, with the French armies in blue and the combined Austro-Russian forces in red. The weak French right wing was to lure opponents into attacking from the dominating Pratzen Heights (at right), while the bulk of the French army launched its main attack on the weakened centre of the Austro-Russian lines.

blanketed in a dense fog which Napoleon had seen on previous mornings and worked into his battle plan. The Allies, however, had made no such provision and suffered badly in the fog as they tried to establish their columns.

The battle site was six miles (10km) long, north to south – an area full of small hills and streams, bordered on the south by shallow lakes. Small villages and enclosures dotted the landscape. The allies intended to attack first and hit the French right wing, pushing it back towards the north, while a secondary action would neutralize the French left wing.

In his military career Napoleon followed one of three main principles: penetration of the enemy lines; attacking the enemy's central position then destroying the divided forces; or, most often, enveloping his enemy and attacking on the flank or at the rear. The latter had worked at Ulm but the second tactic was the key to Austerlitz. He had made himself seem deliberately weak in the south, to lure the Allies to attack there. When they had done so he would launch his attack, with troops he had deliberately hidden in the fog, against the enemy centre around the Pratzen Heights.

At 5 a.m. Napoleon gave his last orders to his marshals. At 6 a.m. the allied right wing was virtually immobile but the left wing attacked at Telnitz. After an hour of

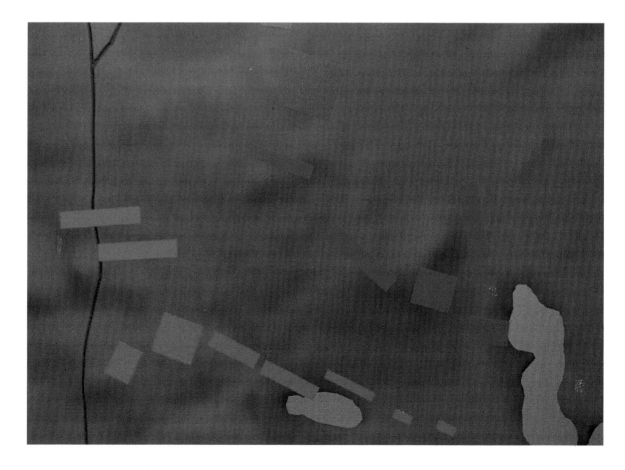

Napoleon's armies facing their opponents ranged across the Pratzen Heights.

fighting the French were given explicit orders to retreat and allow the Austrians to advance. Due to the fog and problems of combined Austro-Russian command, the cohesion of this attack faltered. The motivation of the Allied forces waned in the confusion. One corps of cavalry had even camped on the wrong side of the Pratzen Heights and had to rush north, obstructing infantry moving south. The French also suffered in the fog and some men were shot by their own troops.

Napoleon had relied on the Allies to attack his flanks. Kutusov had argued that the Austro-Russians should be cautious in attacking there but he had been overruled, ultimately by the Russian Tsar and Austrian Emperor who interfered when they should have observed. Napoleon, as he had hoped, drew 50,000 men to his southern right wing, where only 16,000 Frenchmen opposed them. It was now the turn of the French to act. On the battlefield the basic methods of communication were the human voice, trumpet, drum, fires and flares. One such signal was sent to a division of troops under Davout on the far right whose soldiers had been hiding behind a hill; these were now to make their assault.

By 8.45 a.m. Napoleon was ready for his hidden troops to attack, but timing was crucial and he waited another fifteen minutes to be sure that the allies were occupied elsewhere. In his head, every move was calculated and every action and result assimilated. Napoleon's tactical skill (which was far from faultless on other occasions) was in knowing when to play his move and with what.

As church bells rang out nine o'clock, Napoleon turned to his officers and ordered the attack: 'One sharp blow and the war's over.' At this very moment a huge red sun emerged, magnified by the dense fog, and gave birth to the legend of the 'sun of Austerlitz'. The drums beat out the 'pas de charge' and Davout's divisions,

Tsar Alexander I of Russia. After the battle of Austerlitz, Alexander sent this message for Napoleon: 'Tell your master that I am going away. Tell him that he has performed miracles . . . that the battle has increased my respect for him; that he is a man predestined by Heaven; that it will require a hundred years for my army to equal his.'

encouraged by a round of alcohol, moved forward. The Battle of the Three Emperors, as it came to be known, had entered a vital phase.

Kutusov had been relatively content with how things were progressing – his left wing was slowly getting the better of the French – until someone shouted: 'My God, look there! There, just below us – those are Frenchmen!' Kutusov was shocked; the Pratzen Heights were under attack and he knew this centre had to be supported immediately. He ordered any troops still heading south to turn and help him. It was too late. By 11 a.m. the French had taken the Heights and caused heavy allied casualties.

However, Kutusov was far from beaten. He launched retaliatory attacks to regain the Heights. But, firing artillery at point-blank range, the French pushed them back. At midday, Napoleon himself moved his command post and his Imperial Guard on to the Pratzen.

To the north of the field, an almost separate battle was underway between French and Austro-Russian cavalries. The crash of polished armour as both sides engaged could be heard across the fields.

The allies made one last-ditch attempt to take the Pratzen using the Russian Imperial Guard and at 1 p.m. launched an all-out attack from behind the slopes. They managed to reach the summit, smashing through the French front lines before withdrawing to reform. Shortly after, the Russians sent in their Imperial Guard cavalry and Napoleon could do nothing to stop French troops fleeing past him. He had to act rapidly under great pressure to prevent a reversal. He brought up some of his reserve cavalry, which went into immediate action against the Russians. It was a bloody and desperate battle, only decided by the timely arrival of Napoleon's I Corps and more French cavalry. The Russians were thrust back, the panic was over and the battle effectively won. One final French assault on the Allies' remaining forces completed the victory. Orders were given not to take prisoners. Napoleon murmured: 'Many fine ladies of St Petersburg will lament this day.' The armies of the old monarchical Europe had been crushed by the armies of revolution.

By dusk, 36,000 dead and injured – 9,000 French and 27,000 allied – lay upon the blood-soaked fields. Some allied troops lost their lives fleeing across the frozen lakes to the south, which Napoleon is believed to have ordered bombarded to break the ice.

For those Frenchmen who survived, there was glory and Napoleon's appreciation:

Soldiers, I am pleased with you . . . . It will suffice that you shall say: 'I was at the battle of Austerlitz' for them to reply: 'There goes a brave man.'

Tsar Alexander fled while, two days later, Francis of Austria agreed an armistice at the nearby town of Austerlitz. This treaty was eventually signed on the 26 December at Pressburg. Napoleon took lands in Germany and Italy from the Austrians. From the Russians he took little as he wished to cultivate the Tsar's friendship. In Germany he created the Confederation of the Rhine with sixteen reigning princes and kings. The Bourbon Kings of the Two Sicilies were evicted and the crown given to Napoleon's brother Joseph. Another brother, Louis, became King of Holland. One family ruled virtually half the continent.

Austerlitz was Napoleon's first battle in over five years and the first full test of his Grande Armée. His reputation as a great commander had been fully established. In France, his popularity reached new heights; he could do no wrong, though he had failed to secure the peace he had promised. He seemed unable to treat those he had defeated in any manner other than as second-rate losers. In this respect, he lacked Alexander the Great's sure touch. But so long as the wars could be won, why worry too much about the peace?

In September 1806, Prussia declared war on France but was massively defeated at Jena and Auerstadt. In the same year Napoleon turned on Britain again. He had imposed a continental blockade in an effort to destroy the British economy, but Portugal refused to comply, forcing Napoleon to declare war in late 1807. He sent his troops via Spain but a rapid deterioration of the relationship between the Spanish King and Napoleon led to insurrection against French troops. The old dynasty was deposed and the throne given to Napoleon's brother.

Casualties of battle, by Vigneron, Musée Carnavalet, Paris

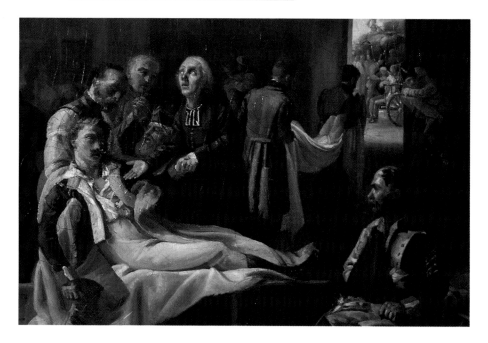

The revolts spread through Spain and for seven years, 1807-14, Napoleon's forces had to fight throughout the Iberian peninsula. Napoleon went to Spain in person in 1808 and chased a small British force almost all the way to the sea but then left the country to his marshals. None of these, however, could end the long guerilla war or defeat the British General Wellington. In Spain, slowly and at a cost of millions of francs, Napoleon lost an army of 220,000 men and inadvertently opened a route for the eventual invasion of France.

Napoleon had been more concerned with central Europe and had defeated the Russians and Prussians again in 1807 and the Austrians once more in 1809. By 1810 his empire was at its greatest extent. Desperate for an heir, he divorced his first wife Josephine (by whom he had no children) and married Marie-Louise, daughter of his Austerlitz adversary, Francis II of Austria. (Napoleon also hoped the marriage would secure Francis as an ally.) A son was born in 1811 and immediately designated King of Rome. A new dynasty had been born.

Napoleon's downfall was accelerated by his decision to invade Russia. 'It was amazing that although Napoleon's common sense amounted to genius, he never quite knew where the possible left off' (*Mollien*). He raised an army of 650,000 but the Tsar called his bluff and retreated, drawing Napoleon further and further into the heart of Russia. As the Russians retreated, they burnt the land and, despite enormous pre-planning, food began to run out. Napoleon reached Moscow itself but his arrival there made little difference. The opposition, instead of suing for peace, had left their city on fire. Despite victories at Smolensk on 17 August 1812 and against his old adversary Kutusov at Borodino on 7 September, Napoleon could not win a decisive victory. Russia had shown the beginnings of what was to become known as 'total war'.

The Russian campaign turned into a disaster. Napoleon had spent a great deal of effort arranging supplies for this campaign and had taken unprecedented steps to provide rations. But the forward distribution from the main depots broke down totally. Eastern Europe was too sparsely populated and badly farmed to allow Napoleon's army to simply 'live off the land'.

> . . . we have received no meat nor vegetables; so that from hunger thirty men killed ourselves a dog and have picked nettles and have cooked us a greenery dish with the dog's fat and eaten the meat for much hunger, for in the Polish lands there is so little to live on. (*Wilhelm Figner*)

Napoleon was forced to retreat, and as the army did so tens of thousands died:

> When we came nearer the Beresina river, there was a place where Napoleon ordered his pack horses to be unharnessed and where he ate. He watched his army pass by in the most wretched condition. What he may have felt in his heart is impossible to surmise. His outward appearance seemed indifferent and unconcerned over the wretchedness of his soldiers; only ambition and lost honour may have made themselves felt in his heart. (*Jakob Walter*)

The Grande Armée retreats from Russia, by Rochling. As rations ran out, desperate soldiers turned to looting their own supply wagons.

Of the 650,000 men who set out, only 75,000 survived. It was a catastrophe (and one that Hitler should have paid more heed to). In early December, Napoleon rushed back to Paris where he had heard that a coup attempt had been launched against him. Once his position was secured, he rapidly organized a new army and rushed back to fight the oncoming enemy. A German campaign followed in 1813 but Napoleon was now heavily outnumbered by the Russians, Austrians and Prussians. The nationalism that had infused French troops to such an extent had become equally potent in the countries of his adversaries. Despite his best efforts, Napoleon was overwhelmed at Leipzig (the Battle of Nations) between 16-19 October 1813 and was forced back over the French frontier. Napoleon's last-ditch battles lost hundreds of thousands more troops.

In early 1814, he won time with a series of small but brilliantly timed blows against his pursuers. This made him seem set, if not exactly to regain the initiative, at least to stave off total defeat. By now, however, his enemies sensed his demise was imminent and pushed him all the way to Paris. Napoleon had no choice but to abdicate at Fontainbleau where he tried to take poison. He was exiled to the Mediterranean island of Elba.

Napoleon was ruler of Elba but it was too small and he was unable to stifle his own ambition. Only forty-five years old, in mid-1814 he sought to return to former glories. Although many French people had tired of their war-mongering emperor, they were just as unwilling to see the return of the monarchy. When a ragbag of exiled courtiers reappeared in France and acted as though the Revolution had never happened, the way lay open for Napoleon to make one last gamble.

Napoleon escaped from Elba and sailed to Fréjus near Cannes, arriving on 1 March 1815. He then marched inland and rallied the local populace to his aid; near Grenoble he won over the soldiers sent to arrest him. By 20 March, he was back in Paris and *de facto* ruler once more. Napoleon knew he needed a major victory to secure his position and hurried north. On 16 June he defeated the Prussians at Ligny, and Marshal Ney held Wellington to a draw at Quatre-Bras.

Napoleon expected the Prussians to fall back to Germany. When he moved to destroy the cornered British at Waterloo on 18 June 1815, he was therefore confident of securing a famous victory. Wellington's stout resistance and the Prussians' timely arrival, however, resulted in an envelopment – one of Napoleon's own favourite manoeuvres – from which he could not extricate his forces. Both his army and his career were destroyed.

The victorious allies exiled Napoleon again, this time to St Helena in the mid-Atlantic. After six arduous years during which he dictated his reminiscences, he died in 1821, aged fifty-two, possibly of poisoning.

Almost as soon as he died, his legend began to grow to almost ridiculous proportions. Books and pamphlets flooded the market. In December 1840, a magnificent funeral was held in Paris and Napoleon's body was returned from St Helena, conveyed through the Arc de Triomphe and magnificently entombed in Les Invalides.

Napoleon was probably the single most powerful man that lived before the twentieth century. Yet, until his death, he consistently demanded as much of himself as of any of his subordinates. It was not wealth or respect that he craved nor was it glory for France. Napoleon sought challenge; he dared anyone to out-think him. The bullying of his youth must have left a deep imprint on him, for, throughout his life, Napoleon sought to dominate, to crush, to belittle all of those with whom he sought conflict.

In his wars he lost an estimated 2,500,000 men dead and showed little sorrow at having done so. He was ruthless, self-centred and arrogant, and yet had the ability to make his men love him even while he sent them to their deaths. He could lead men where lesser generals could not. But casualties are most generally overlooked when dealing with Napoleon; it is the memory of his skills and successes that have excited future generations.

Longwood House, Napoleon's last home. His family were not allowed to join him in St Helena. The former Emperor spent his remaining years in the simple plantation house attended by a miniature court, dictating his memoirs and replanting the gardens, under the strict supervision of the British governor, Sir Hudson Lowe.

CHAPTER FIVE

ULYSSES S. GRANT

'I can not spare him – he fights!' (Lincoln)

At the outbreak of the American Civil War Ulysses S. Grant was an ill-paid shop clerk – within four years he was commanding general of the Union Army, and within seven he was President of the United States.

In the bloody civil war, Grant showed many of the qualities of a great commander: he was tenacious, determined and, most of all, understood that war was not about battles but campaigns. Casualties were high – some called him a butcher – but Grant's great asset was that he saw that war not only took place in a military sphere, but also had political, social, economic and diplomatic elements.

At the Battle of the Wilderness, Grant, having led his army into a devilish entanglement of trees and bushes, faced an opponent who both knew the land and was waiting for him. The battle was an engagement in which his troops suffered badly and yet Grant knew that the gain lay not in individual engagements but in the outcome of the war.

Hiram Ulysses Grant was born in the small town of Point Pleasant, Ohio, on 27 April 1822, the son of Jesse and Hannah. Life was tough and Ulysses was soon helping out in his father's tannery and on their small farm. In 1839 Jesse arranged for his son to go to the United States Military Academy at West Point. When he arrived there, he decided to enrol as Ulysses Hiram Grant to avoid the potentially embarrassing initials of H.U.G. This was incorrectly written down as Ulysses Simpson (his mother's maiden name) and as military records are virtually impossible to change, the name stuck: U. S. Grant.

Grant wrote in his biography that, on entering the Academy, he was devoid of military ambition:

Ulysses Simpson Grant.

A military life had no claims for me and I had not the faintest idea of staying in the army, even if I should be graduated, which I did not expect.

His parents had been attracted by the free education and respected academic curriculum but Grant preferred novels to textbooks. Nevertheless, by the end of the course, he had decided to become a college professor of mathematics.

Grant graduated in 1843, twenty-first of thirty-nine (from an original class of seventy-six) and instead of college, he joined the infantry. In 1844, he was sent to Texas.

The United States of America was at this time experiencing rapid, sometimes painful, change. Throughout the country, but especially in the north, which had a population of 28 million, advances in transportation and communication such as the telegraph and railroad helped to create a national economic framework and change this Union of States into a unified nation. The southern states, however, with their

Grant as a young officer in 1843.

smaller population of 9 million (4 million of whom were slaves) began to resent its northern neighbours. Tensions grew. In the South, slavery was the backbone of the economy. Large plantations, many growing cotton, needed cheap labour and black slaves provided it. Industrialists in the North, which was substantially wealthier, relied more on trade and industry, manned by wave after wave of European immigrant. The North could afford to follow a more liberal line. In the South, most of the white population, particularly the 350,000 slave-owners, resented being lectured about 'freedom'. The Union began to tear apart.

Slaves at work in the fields of Pope's Plantation near Hilton Head, South Carolina.

In 1845, there was a diversion. The United States invaded Mexico. Grant disapproved of the motives behind this conflict, calling it 'One of the most unjust ever waged by a stronger against a weaker nation . . . . It was an instance of a republic following the bad example of European monarchies.'

Nevertheless, he fought with distinction in four battles, including the battle for Mexico City itself, and showed great initiative. Indeed, he made a name for himself in one assault by using a cannon to bombard a Mexican position from a church tower. After the war, which brought to the Union a huge swathe of land including Arizona, California and New Mexico, Grant served in various posts but, missing his wife Julia, and possibly finding himself increasingly dependent on alcohol, he resigned his commission in 1854. For six years he tried farming, business and real estate but did not have a head for it; his military common sense was not reflected in his commercial ventures. Humbled by defeat, he eventually sought work with his younger brothers in the family tannery. The future was not very bright, but at least, aged thirty-nine with a wife and four children to support, he was earning a steady wage.

A typical Southern plantation house at Beaufort, South Carolina, photographed in 1862.

After the Mexican War, the Union faced the problem of whether the territories acquired during the Mexican War should be admitted as slave states or free states. When Abraham Lincoln, who was against the extension of slavery, was elected President in 1860, the South took it as their signal to secede. Eleven states abandoned the Union (and two others offered their support) and, in the spring of 1861, established their own capital, first in Montgomery, Alabama, and then in Richmond, Virginia under the presidency of Jefferson Davis. Civil war had begun.

First and foremost, the fight, as far as the North was concerned, was to preserve the Union. It was a struggle in which submission of the South would be the only acceptable outcome.

The United States had only a tiny army of about 13,000 troops and officers watching over the frontiers and native Americans. When the war began both sides called for three-month volunteers. This was initially a great success, primarily because many thought the conflict would all be over in a few months. Even after recruitment terms were lengthened to two or three years, regiments were easily formed with eager workers, labourers and farm-boys enthusiastic to see more in their lifetime than just their homes. Within months Union President Lincoln had 400,000 men under arms.

These volunteers from many backgrounds and languages were slow to appreciate the need for drill and discipline. Some had recently fled strict regimes in Europe precisely to avoid such rules and regulations. Neither was there a ready pool of men to lead them: few officers had the necessary skills or experience.

As a West Point graduate, Grant became a useful commodity. He helped drill local volunteers and was asked by the governor to help on his staff. Finally he gained the command of a local group of rough and ready volunteers.

> I saw new energies in him, he dropped a stoop-shouldered way of walking, and set his hat forward on his head in a jaunty fashion.

Grant's first task was to introduce some discipline, through 'the application of a little regular army punishment'.

The Appalachian Mountains cut the war into two primary 'theatres': the western theatre centred around the Mississippi River and its tributaries and the eastern theatre between the northern capital Washington and the southern capital Richmond, only 100 miles (160km) away. The Union had the huge advantage in terms of economic power and a much larger population and its grand strategy was designed to take advantage of them. The Anaconda Plan, as it was called, focused on Richmond, the western rivers and a naval blockade of the South's coasts. It was hoped that by achieving these goals the life would be squeezed out of the rebellious states. The Confederates were the more determined, but their Achilles heel was the very thing they were fighting to preserve: slavery. Not only did they refuse to recruit blacks but they had to station men to

Grant photographed with his son Jesse and his wife, Julia.

protect against black insurgence. Since the South had fewer men and could not send them all to the front line, the North had an immediate advantage.

Grant was fighting not against slavery but for the ideal of 'the Union'. He also fought because it felt good to be needed again. He certainly never gave anyone reason to question his commitment, and, from the very first engagement, despite his own fears, led rather than pushed his troops.

Apart from learning military drill and discipline, Grant's West Point education was hardly relevant. His skill was based on learning from circumstance and experience, an informal school with no fixed doctrine or set ideas. Military training at West Point had been based on the lessons of the Napoleonic wars; even the uniforms and manuals were based on French equivalents. However, these battles of the American Civil War were fought not on large open fields but in tangled woods, over narrow streams and along winding tracks. Most great commanders have native genius which improves with education and experience. Alexander was expertly schooled, and learnt war at his father's side. Caesar was a well-educated member of the minor aristocracy who learned about war as a governor and from his own military mistakes. Nelson learnt from study and experience at sea. Napoleon attended a military school and formulated his ideas in private study, thinking through each concept to form a composite strategy which he tried out on the battlefield. Grant learnt little at West Point, something in Mexico, but most of what he knew as he went along. War itself was his textbook.

Grant's first battle at Belmont, Missouri, on 7 November 1861 was a near-failure. He had secretly planned to seize a Confederate camp near the Mississippi River. Grant, who was a very minor player in the war at this point, briefed his men on the steamer heading for a landing site three miles (5km) from the objective. Once there, Grant led his men through thick forest and took the camp but his troops, having engaged in an orgy of looting, were then caught unprepared by a counter-attack and were pushed back to the boats. Grant regained control and was the last to leave but nothing had been achieved. He had failed to realize that his unwieldy volunteers needed even stricter discipline if success was to be assured. He saw the errors, however, and set about correcting them.

In February 1862, Grant was in command of attacks on Fort Henry on the Tennessee River and Fort Donelson on the Cumberland River, both very important lines of communication. While his coordination between land assault and naval bombardments was poor, and inadequate administration left troops cold and starved of ammunition, Grant's energy and commitment enabled him to take 16,500 prisoners for the loss of only 3,000 Union soldiers:

> His silence is remarkable. He knew how to keep his temper. In battle, as in camp, he went about quietly, speaking in conversational tone; yet he appeared to see everything that went on, and was always intent on business. (*Lew Wallace*)

At Fort Donelson, Grant had demanded unconditional surrender and henceforth earned himself the nickname 'Unconditional Surrender Grant'. For the first time, he rose to national prominence.

The first major civil war engagement in which Grant was involved was the bloody battle of Shiloh, on the Tennessee River, in April 1862. Grant had travelled down river and had sent five of his six divisions ahead to disembark at the Pittsburgh Landing and nearby Shiloh Church while he waited downstream to meet reinforcements. He had little information about the whereabouts of the Confederates under A. S. Johnston, and Grant did not order the use of cavalry reconnaissance.

The Confederate troops knew that Grant was on his way with reinforcements and, a good offence being the best defence, they decided to attack without delay. Their dawn assault on 6 April caught the Union troops completely off guard – many were actually asleep – and the Union line was pushed back two miles (3km). When Grant arrived at the Pittsburgh Landing he was met with the sight of thousands of fugitives either hiding under a bluff or trying to leave.

Grant, despite pain from a riding injury, organized ammunition supplies, redeployed new troops and rode along the front line plugging gaps, offering encouragement and trying to stop the fleeing troops. He asked one soldier, 'What are you running for?' to which the man replied, 'Because I can't fly'.

Despite his efforts, the Union line started to buckle at both ends; only the centre was holding. Grant's forces faced a complete rout if the centre failed as there was nothing but river behind them; but the centre held for a long, vital period until a final line of defences was established near the river. After desperate fighting, the Confederates eventually broke through and advanced. By nightfall, however, with Johnston mortally

Union paddlesteamers moored at Pittsburg Landing. The second boat from the right is the Tigress, *Grant's floating headquarters during the battle of Shiloh.*

wounded, the Confederates had been unable to break Grant's last line. Both exhausted armies rested, the Confederates sure of victory in the morning.

That night Sherman came across Grant standing under a tree, away from the screams of the wounded. It was raining and he was smoking a cigar to keep warm. 'Well, Grant, we've had the devil's own day, haven't we?' 'Yep,' said Grant, drawing on his cigar. 'Lick 'em tomorrow though.'

During the night, Union reinforcements arrived and when fighting resumed in the morning the Confederates were, to their surprise, forced back. By 4 p.m. the Union troops had regained their original position but did not pursue. Grant had not the heart to send his men on, after they had just spent two days fighting in mud and rain – an act of lenience for which he was later reprimanded.

Casualties at Shiloh were very high – 13,500 Union troops and 10,500 Confederates – but the moral victory belonged to the Union. Grant was blamed, however, for not preparing against the surprise attack or consolidating an even greater victory. Some criticism is justified, but his behaviour during the battle was outstanding. He visited every divisional commander in turn, and inspired them with his own determination. He was a rock of strength in a frightening, messy battle of attrition. He was one of the very few who seemed to have the courage to accept that war was murderous but had to be fought as such and not shied away from:

Panoramic view of the town of Vicksburg, a trading centre for cotton on the Mississippi River.

[He] habitually wears an expression as if determined to drive his head through a brick wall and was about to do it. (*Union soldier*)

The Battle of Vicksburg, 19 May 1863, from the painting by H. Charles McBarron. Despite the heroic image, and the eventual surrender of the besieged Confederates, Union soldiers were slaughtered by the hundred in spirited but futile direct assaults on Vicksburg's defences.

At the end of 1862, Grant, now in charge of the Armies of the Tennessee and Mississippi, began an advance on Vicksburg, one of the last major Confederate strongholds on the Mississippi River. The capture of the town would effectively secure Union control of this vital river, thus splitting the Confederacy in two and depriving its troops of important supplies and reinforcements.

Vicksburg was a considerable fortress, nicknamed 'America's Gibraltar', sitting on a 200-foot (61m) bluff on the eastern bank of the Mississippi. The area around the town itself was staunchly defended by a strong Confederate force. On the opposite bank the swampy forest was all but impassable. The fortress had artillery directed at the river, thus making it highly dangerous for any Union boats attempting to pass.

Grant's plan has become a classic campaign, studied today at West Point as an example to young officers. Grant had tried to reach Vicksburg from the north but the topography was unfavourable. He therefore determined to approach from the south, and thus surprise the Confederates. This was, however, a very complicated operation. Grant had to bring his outnumbered troops down the Mississippi, disembark them and march along the west bank through swamp and forest opposite Vicksburg, until they were safely to the south of the city. With great daring, the transport ships next had to run the gauntlet of Vicksburg's artillery fire in order to rejoin Grant and ferry his troops back across the river. Union forces then moved north-east to take Jackson. Having achieved this objective, they turned due west and headed for Vicksburg. The plan to capture the town was so risky and irregular because it involved abandoning lines of supply and living off the land. It was a major departure from everything that had been taught at West Point and few, if any, other generals would have dared consider it, never mind implement it. Grant realized that this war was different:

Some of our generals failed because they worked out everything by rule . . . .
They were always thinking about what would Napoleon do. Unfortunately for
their plans, the rebels would be thinking about something else.

Equal measures of determination and resilience nevertheless led Grant to success. He made the happy discovery that the countryside was so well stocked that his
troops could live adequately, despite the miserable conditions in the muddy marshes.
Grant did not have particularly accurate maps and did not know the country. His own
side thought he would not succeed; indeed, his superiors' advice was not to try. No
one could have conceived of doing what Grant did; to live off the land in this way was
totally new. The Confederates tried to prevent the advance but, in the end, they were
forced to retreat within the fortress and prepare for siege.

On arrival at the defences of Vicksburg, Grant's troops were hot and tired and in no
mood to dig in: they wanted an immediate attack. Grant could see the dangers posed by
the four-mile (6km) line of entrenchments but nevertheless gave his troops the order to
do so. Two direct assaults failed and Grant reverted to besieging the town. He refused
to allow civilians to leave, despite their increasing hunger: Grant saw war as peoples
against peoples. A month and a half later, on 4 July, Vicksburg hoisted the white flag.

Grant agreed to the surrender, in spite of the objections raised by his generals in
the only council of war ever held. Under the terms of surrender the Confederates
were allowed to go home on condition that they did not bear arms again. In doing
this, Grant was already displaying an overriding awareness that the war was being
fought for political ends: he wanted to deflate Confederate commitment and he was
considering the post-war implications of his actions.

President Lincoln had kept watch on the general in the west and was impressed
not only with Grant's victories but also with his apparent lack of interest in intrigue or
political office. This was the kind of commander that he had been waiting for, one
who would take responsibility for the job and not expect Lincoln to have the final
word or responsibility: 'I'm glad to find a man who can go ahead without me.'

*'I claim not to have con-
trolled events, but con-
fess plainly that events
have controlled me.'
Abraham Lincoln,
1864.*

On 3 March 1864, Grant was summoned to Washington and was made the new
Union commanding general. Lincoln's three previous commanding generals had all
proved cautious, ineffective and often reluctant to move swiftly into battle and fight to
the bitter end. Grant was different – and Lincoln knew it. One day he received a com-
plaint that Grant drank too much whisky, to which Lincoln replied, 'Send all my other
generals a crate of the same brand!'

Grant lost no time. Within weeks he had fought his first battle: the Battle of the
Wilderness. It was a brief but intense conflict, illustrating four great characteristics of
Grant's command abilities: his understanding of strategy and the role each campaign
plays within that strategy; his tenacity and determination; his composure in battle;
and his inspirational character.

The presidential election was to be held in the autumn and the politicking had
begun. Lincoln was under severe pressure and considered it likely he would lose to

McClellan, an opposing candidate running on a peace platform. Families had suffered heartache and industry had been badly hit by the war. The press, playing an important role in warfare for one of the first times, were as critical as they were complimentary. Many troops were at the end of their three-year service and unlikely to extend their terms of service. New recruits were hard to come by and those who had volunteered back in 1861 – by now the best troops – were being depleted day by day through casualties. Bitterness was growing against those who stayed in the rear, and seemed better paid. For many, the appeal of a military life had faded long before and the Union armies were finding it increasingly difficult to maintain the manning levels they were used to. The Union had no choice but to introduce the draft. That increased the sense of unease felt in the North towards the war. Parents and sons alike were beginning to wonder whether it was all worthwhile. By the autumn of 1864, Grant also thought the war had lasted too long. But he wanted to finish it by defeating the enemy, not signing by an armistice with them.

Robert E. Lee. Although he supported the preservation of the Union and opposed slavery, Lee felt that his first loyalty was to his home state of Virginia, which seceded in April 1861. His large estate overlooking Washington was confiscated in 1864 and the grounds became the Arlington National Cemetary.

He immediately set to work on strategy for victory. He realized that politics dominates strategy as much as geography dominates tactics. His strategy was to use his numerical advantage to apply uniform pressure against the south, inflict losses and prevent the redeployment of troops between Confederate armies. Grant was no longer in charge of just one army but now had 500,000 men and an entire campaign to organize. There were a number of participating armies but many were small or peripheral. The two most important were Sherman's force (against Confederate General E. Johnston's army), which would head for Atlanta in the west, and General G. Meade's Army of the Potomac (like all Union armies, named after a river), which would attempt to destroy Lee's Army of North Virginia.

> Before this time these various armies had acted separately and independently of each other . . . I determined to stop this. (*Grant*)

The key to the operations in the east was to wear down Lee's army. Grant declared: 'I look upon the conquering of the organized armies of the enemy as being vastly more important than the mere acquisition of their territory.' Grant explained this to Lincoln who was enthusiastic but told Grant to keep all the details secret and not to tell even him. There must be no chance of Lee becoming aware of Union intentions.

Grant had no interest in staying in Washington and he left the administrative detail to others, namely Halleck, (the Chief-of-Staff), Stanton, (the Secretary of War) and Lincoln. He travelled there once a week for meetings but that was enough. (On one trip Grant came perilously close to being caught by Confederate partisans working behind the lines.) The President had promised not to interfere but political demands sometimes made him go back on that pledge. One result was that he insisted on the appointment of three less-talented commanders to direct subsidiary manoeuvres. These commanders – Butler, Siegel and Banks – were political appointments made by Lincoln to keep various state governors happy. Grant had no choice but to work with

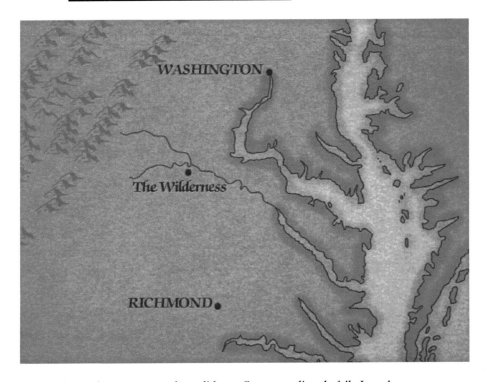

The site of the Wilderness, mid-way between the Federal capital of Washington DC, and the rebel Confederate capital of Richmond, Virginia.

George Meade was a stubborn and somewhat unpopular general but he worked well with Grant, who accompanied the Army of the Potomac, which Meade commanded, during the Wilderness campaign.

them. These three commanders did, as Grant predicted, fail. Lee, however, never managed to take advantage of this Union weakness – Grant did not let him.

Grant knew that his place was among his men. In the west, Sherman was the commander in whom Grant had the greatest confidence and who was left to his own devices. In the eastern theatre, however, Grant did not know the commanders and their record was poor. Grant travelled with Meade's Army of the Potomac and camped with it. Although he left the basic tactical decisions to Meade, Grant constantly kept his eye on him and occasionally issued orders to Meade's subordinates without consulting him. To some extent, this diminished Grant's wider perspective of the war but he had no choice; destroying Lee was the number one aim and he could not afford to fail. A move towards Richmond was thus used as bait to make Lee come out and fight.

Grant told Meade that he was to follow and harass Lee without respite: '. . . wherever Lee's army goes, you will go also.' Grant tried to make Meade's job easier by coordinating Meade's actions with those of General Butler, who was to attack Richmond from the south. Once Meade and Butler's forces were acting in unison, Grant felt sure the Confederacy would fall.

The Army of the Potomac was ordered to cross a stretch of land called the Wilderness in order to pass the right flank of Lee's army, dug in near the south bank of the Rapidan River. Grant hoped he would get through before engaging Lee but he would fight him wherever he attacked. He felt confident that his 116,000 men would defeat Lee's 61,000.

Having arrived at the winter quarters of the Army of the Potomac, Grant enforced both drilling and target practice, and organized supplies. A central part of Grant's strategy was the ability for the army to be able to remain on campaign indefinitely. There was to be no returning north for supplies, everything went with them. The Union always had the advantage because of its economic strength, whereas the Confederates increasingly struggled to feed their troops. Grant wanted to heighten the disruption of enemy supplies; the state of Georgia, for example, a key source of food, transportation and industrial goods, was high on his list of targets. Despite the Union's advantages, skill was still required to see that the right supplies reached the right troops at the right time. Grant's experiences in other campaigns had made him fully aware of the difficulties involved and, more importantly, some of their solutions.

In preparation for the Wilderness campaign he saw to it that there were ten days' rations, forage and ammunition in wagons. Each of Grant's soldiers had three days' rations in his haversack along with forty or fifty rounds of cartridges. Grant wrote to Halleck that he needed 'one million rations and two hundred forage rations afloat to be sent wherever it may prove they will be required'. Beef cattle were driven along and butchered as required.

Steam power had changed logistics. Not only were railroads available but it was now possible to travel upstream along rivers. Without these new methods of transport the war could not have been fought as it was; the distances were too great. A

Disruption of the railway system to prevent supplies reaching the front line was a strategy used by both sides in the war. Army engineers worked at incredible speed to rebuild destroyed bridges with elaborate wooden structures.

Supply wagons stretch into the distance, as Grant's army advances towards the Wilderness across the Rapidan River in the spring of 1864.

single railroad could do the work of tens of thousands of wagons. Protecting communications thus became one of the central tasks of the war.

Grant relied on sea and river transport to furnish his bases with supplies, and the roads – poor as they were – to supply his troops. As he had no intention of stopping or retreating, he had to have a large enough baggage train to supply him for weeks, even months: 116,000 troops need an enormous quantity of material. The result was a convoy of 4,000 wagons, so many that Grant estimated that, tail to tail, it would have stretched 60-70 miles (97–113km).

On the eve of his departure, Grant wrote to his wife:

I know the greatest anxiety is now felt in the north for the success of this move
. . . I feel well myself. Do not know whether this is any criterion from which to judge results because I have never felt otherwise . . . unless indeed it has been when thrown in strange company, particularly of ladies. (*Grant*)

A little past midnight on 4 May, they set out. For once, Grant, who normally wore simple, almost tatty clothes with the general's insignia pinned on his shoulder, dressed

up. This was something special. The convoy lumbered south. Grant had no choice but to head through the Wilderness: to the west and the east the ground was unsuitable or the river too wide. Engineers, protected by cavalry, led the way in order to build bridges to replace those destroyed by the Confederates. The supply train was so long the army had to move along parallel roads and thus needed a number of crossing points over the Rapidan River, the two most important were at Ely's Ford and Germanna Ford.

The Wilderness stretched for about fifteen miles (24km) west to east and ten miles (16km) north to south. Most trees had been cut down to fuel a nearby iron smelting plant and all that was left, apart from young thin pines, were tangled thickets, bush and new undergrowth. It was a dreadful place for battle, almost impenetrable by light, let alone line troops. Barely a year before, Union troops had been severely beaten by Lee at nearby Chancellorsville and some of Grant's troops marched past the bones of the dead, which lay where they had fallen:

> . . . half-open graves, displaying arms and legs with bits of paling and mildewed clothing still clinging to them: – oh, war's glory, this is your reverse side! (*Schaff*)

Here in the Wilderness there was no place for massed troops manoeuvring in perfect order. This was 'skirmish' country, wherein men made use of every hollow, every tree. The landscape defined the battle and the commanders did their best to operate within these restrictive conditions. Often a commander could see no more than a few of his troops in action; he, like everyone else, had to guess what was happening from the sounds around him and wait patiently for news.

It was a wrestle as blind as at midnight, a gloom that made manoeuvres impracticable, a jungle where regiments stumbled on each other and on the enemy in turns, firing sometimes into their own ranks, and guided often only by the crackling of the bushes or cheers and cries that rose from the depths around. (*Badeau*)

Lee had decided that it would be unwise to attempt to meet Grant head-on or even try to stop him crossing the river, which was quite low. His plan was to lure Grant into the Wilderness and there try to defeat him. So he waited. The improved quality of rifles was a crucial component of the warfare seen in the American Civil War. Smoothbore muskets could only fire 100 yards (90m) but the new rifled muskets could now fire 800 yards (730m) with some accuracy, putting an end to cavalry charges and leading to the introduction of trench warfare. As soon as troops arrived at a new position they would set to work with spades and axes digging in and protecting their fronts with trees and branches. Such defences could be fired from, but only by extreme luck could a bullet penetrate in the other direction. The defenders had the advantage.

The opposing armies in the Wilderness on the morning of 6 May, with Grant's superior forces in blue.

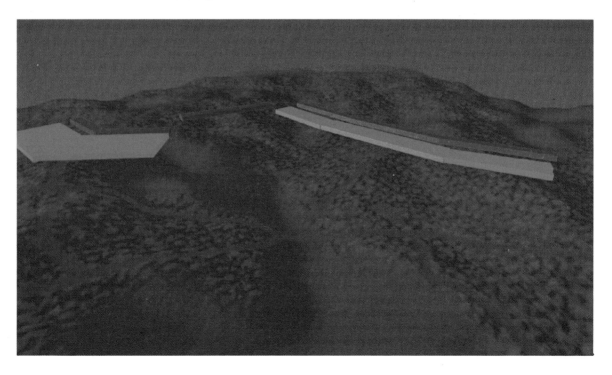

Although Grant hoped to get through the Wilderness so that he could fight Lee on open ground, he was willing to fight the Confederates anywhere. He knew that Lee did not have the capacity to launch an attack on Washington. On the evening of the 4th, Grant had to call a halt to his advancing front-line troops to give the baggage train a chance to catch up. He ordered his men to set up their bivouacs and await orders. They had no idea that they were sleeping within a few miles of Lee's soldiers.

The next morning dawned hot and humid. Grant ordered the advance to continue. Soon Meade sent a message that some of Lee's troops had been sighted. Although he presumed that these were only a few left behind to guard the road, Meade nevertheless halted the advance.

Suddenly, Lee attacked. The battle that followed centred largely on both the Orange Turnpike and Orange Plank Road, east-west roads that crossed the Wilderness. They were narrow and uneven roads, little more than widened trails, crossed by the north-south Brock Road. Hemmed in with trees, they were dark and eerie. The battle divided itself into almost separate engagements alongside these two roads – an indecisive but bloody battle on and beside the Turnpike, and a more fluid confrontation a couple of miles to the south along the Plank Road.

Trains of supply wagons maintained the Union army's lines of communication across the Southern states.

The tangled undergrowth of the Wilderness, with trees shattered by gunfire after the battle.

The fighting was so fierce that soldiers often saw nothing but the results of bullets ripping into both foliage and flesh. The screams of the wounded, some of whom were burning to death in the numerous small forest fires the fighting had caused, reverberated through the woods. Despite the horror and the casualties, Grant was not going to disengage. The Union troops would fight until the Confederates could fight no more. Grant was not an imaginative leader but he was resolute, even ruthless, and fully aware that the Union could absorb casualties for a longer period than the Confederates. In a war of attrition the larger army should win. 'Grant doesn't care a snap if men fall like the leaves fall; he fights to win, that chap does . . . he has the disagreeable habit of not retreating before irresistible veterans' (*Mary Chestnut*).

While one of Meade's divisions stopped advancing along the Plank Road, to the north the battle raged in the wood and shrub beside the Turnpike. The numerical advantage of Grant's artillery was much reduced by the terrain and both sides soon needed reinforcements. Grant sent for Burnside's troops (which were under Grant's direct control rather than Meade's) and ordered them to the Plank.

Lee, meanwhile, ordered his reserves, under Longstreet, to hurry. By dusk, with few Confederate reinforcements having arrived, the Union troops had come within reach of victory on the Plank Road, but darkness prevented a final push from being made.

The confused fighting ebbed and flowed along and beside the two roads. In such claustrophobic conditions, the closeness of the dense woodland greatly increased by noise and smoke, each man could rarely see more than a few yards around him. As such they were often isolated from direct command. Nevertheless, throughout this highly complex engagement, Grant acted with great skill. First, his coolness under pressure and his skill in taking rapid, clearly expressed decisions proved vital in such a confusing battle. He could not see what was going on and could not take part. All he could do was wait for reports at his command headquarters in a field near Meade's camp. Whether the news was good or bad, whether the noise of battle was close or not, he remained calm and collected:

> He would at times walk slowly up and down, but most of the day he sat upon the stump of a tree, or on the ground, with his back leaning against a tree . . . a lighted cigar was in his mouth almost constantly, and his penknife was kept in active use whittling sticks. (*Porter*)

Grant standing by his command post: 'He habitually wears an expression as if determined to drive his head through a brick wall and was about to do it'

Even today, the remains of trenches scar the lush woodland of the Wilderness.

At one moment, a frightened subordinate rushed up to him and declared that Lee was about to get between them and the Rapidan. Grant calmly responded:

I am heartily tired of hearing about what Lee is going to do. . . . Go back to your command, and try to think what we are going to do ourselves.

Once, asked the secret of his command, Grant replied: 'Find out where your enemy is, get at him as soon as you can and strike him as hard as you can and keep moving on.' When he gave an order, it was always precise. He realized that orders and counter-orders only lead to disorder. When he sat in his tent working, he would write out orders on a piece of paper, then push it off the edge of the table. As the

evening wore on, the pile would grow until he finished. Then he would gather up the pages, hand them to one of his few aides and get them sent off. He had no reason to check them and no one had reason to query the instructions. They were unambiguous. The problem at the Wilderness was that such orders could take hours to reach their destination, so dense was the terrain. It might then take just as long again before the subordinate could follow through the orders.

During the evening, Grant discussed his plans for the following day with his staff and officers. He wanted an attack at 4.30 a.m. but Meade preferred 6 a.m. to give his men more time to rest. Grant, ever aware of maintaining a good relationship with Meade, compromised and agreed to a 5 a.m. start. Grant left Meade with one final

Despite the formality of the pose, Grant's staff meetings were remarked upon as exceptionally relaxed affairs.

order: 'If any opportunity presents itself for pitching into a part of Lee's army, do so without giving time for disposition.'

The attack next morning began well for the Union. They drove the Confederates back to a small clearing in which Lee had his command post. The Union troops had, however, lost much of their cohesion as they had scrambled through the underbrush. Before they had a chance to regroup, the front ranks of Longstreet's reinforcements had finally arrived and opened fire. Lee himself tried to lead his men from the front but his troops shouted for him to get back, out of danger. Lee was one of the last generals who thought he should command from the front line; Grant was one of the first of a new era in which the commander directed from behind the lines.

The Confederates now launched their own attack along an unfinished railway cutting on the Union's left flank and pushed the Union troops back to their defences at the intersection of the Plank and Brock roads but Longstreet was accidentally shot through the throat and the attack was halted.

At 3 p.m. there was a lull and Grant ordered Burnside to hit the Confederates on their left flank on the Plank Road front. This attack was too slow, partly as troops had great difficulty getting through the undergrowth. Meanwhile Lee launched another attack on the Brock-Plank intersection. He fared well and managed to exert heavy pressure on the defences but was unable to breach them and the attack faded out.

Further north, along the Turnpike, the Confederates had found their way around the right flank of the Union lines and, surprised to find it weak, rolled it up with relative ease. But little came of it except the capture of a few hundred prisoners, darkness saving the remaining Union troops from a similar or worse outcome.

Although Grant was not one to address his troops and deliver oratorical masterpieces, he nevertheless inspired his forces. Above all, it was Grant's decision on 7 May that really made the difference, not only to his army but to the war. Union armies had moved towards Richmond on a handful of other occasions and each time they had retreated. Many of the troops in the Army of the Potomac did not know at first who Grant was and were undecided before the Wilderness as to their opinion of him. They tended to believe that Grant's successes in the west had probably been won against weaker opposition than they had been facing in the east. Had Grant, they wondered, ever fought against anyone as expert as Lee?

Grant had decided that the battle of the Wilderness had run its course and he did not want to attack a defensive position again – Lee was too strong and the casualties would be too high. He decided instead to out flank Lee, and by getting between him and Richmond, draw the Confederates out into the open. At 6.30 a.m. Grant ordered Meade to prepare to continue southwards.

During the day, many troops received no information but that night, as they reached the crossroads of the Orange Plank and Brock Road, they received their

Company I of the 57th Massachusetts went into the fighting in the Wilderness on May 6 with eighty-six men. Several weeks later, these nine men were the only survivors.

orders – they were not to turn and head back but to continue on, to the nearby town of Spottsylvania, and confront Lee once again. Although this meant more fighting, the Union troops were overjoyed:

> Soldiers weary and sleepy after their long battle, with stiffened limbs and smarting wounds, now sprang to their feet, forgetful of their pains, and rushed forward to the roadside. Wild cheers echoed through the forest. (*Horace Porter*)

Whereas a commander such as Meade might well have turned back, Grant carried on. His stubbornness and resolution was not going to allow Lee time to regroup or, crucially, redeploy any troops to aid other Confederate armies elsewhere.

Both sides had suffered heavy casualties, the Union especially. But, although tactically the battle may have been indecisive, strategically it was the greatest Union victory won in the eastern theatre. In two days of vicious fighting Lee had been shown that he could not afford to launch fresh offensives. For the rest of the war his strategy would be almost entirely defensive. Thus tied down he could not send troops to

reinforce those fighting the other union thrusts and his final defeat became inevitable. Grant was the first of the modern generals; Lee one of the last from the old school. Grant understood that war was more than individual battles and had to be played out on both the strategic and the political playing fields. For that reason, Lee was to be hounded until he collapsed: 'I propose to fight it out on this line if it takes all summer' (*Grant*).

Days after the Wilderness, Grant and Lee fought again at Spottsylvania and suffered large casualties on both sides. Grant then tried to slip around Lee's right flank and get between him and Richmond. Lee worked out Grant's intentions and set off to intercept, but the Confederates had less distance to cover. On 29 May, with Grant only ten miles (16km) from Richmond, Lee confronted him. Once again, they fought each other to a stalemate.

Grant tried yet again at Cold Harbor in early June. So fatalistic were his troops that they pinned their names on the back of their coats before fighting so that they could be identified in death. Again, the ensuing desperate battle achieved little, other than continuing to wear down Lee and preventing him from releasing reinforcements that could prevent Sherman's move on Atlanta.

Grant had by now decided that the only way to finish the war was to isolate his opponent and simply and slowly, if necessary, wear him down through attrition. To do this he had to cut off any communication west and south by capturing Petersburg, twenty-two miles (35km) south of Richmond, which was the key to the capital's communications with the South's remaining resources.

Soldiers wounded in the Wilderness awaiting treatment at a field hospital. Makeshift hospitals were having to provide basic treatment for thousands of men at a time.

The ruins of Richmond in April 1865, set on fire by retreating Confederate troops. 'We are under the shadow of ruins', wrote one New York reporter. 'From the pavements where we walk . . . stretches a vista of devastation . . . There is no sound of life but the stillness of the catacomb.'

On 16 June, the attack failed and another 10,000 casualties were sustained, but Grant continued to pin down Lee's army. Sherman finally took Atlanta on 4 September, a success that helped secure Lincoln's re-election. The re-election of Lincoln meant the war continued and any hope of armistice was abandoned.

Grant was clearly unable to defeat Lee on the battle field and so settled down into a nine-month siege of Petersburg. Meanwhile, Sherman continued past Atlanta to the sea, wrecking as much of Georgia as he could. By early 1865, Lee's line was in a perilous condition and stretched very thin. His position finally caved in on 1 April and he was forced to evacuate both Richmond and Petersburg and make a run to the west. But the Confederates were cut off (by, among others, one General Custer), and on 9 April 1865 Lee accepted Grant's generous terms of surrender.

The will of the Confederacy had been broken by Grant's tenacity and strategic skills. Lee was made to fight the type of war that he could not win: as long as Grant kept him under pressure, Lee remained highly restricted in the actions he could take, and as he was the leading edge of the Confederate Army, Grant's actions effectively crushed any Southern hopes of victory. Lee had thought he would defeat Grant in the Wilderness but his hope proved unfounded. Although the North grew weary and restless at the manner and expense with which Grant fought, he was nevertheless able to keep Lee in his grip and ultimately secure victory.

Grant knew that victory for the Union would extract a heavy price. Modern weapons meant the end to outmoded tactics and although Grant was as slow as everyone else fully to appreciate the casualties this would lead to, he did recognize that this new, 'modern' warfare contained little of the gentlemanly duels of the past. Peoples fought against one another – military and civilian alike – was involved. At the start of the Civil War day-trippers had picnicked while watching the armies fight. By 1864 there were no by-standers.

Grant has been called a callous leader. Estimates vary, but Union casualties for the entire war were as high as 40 per cent, over half of which were fatalities. For every man who died in battle, two died in sickness. Confederate casualties, however, were even worse, at 60 per cent, again with half of those mortalities. From the Wilderness to the final surrender, Grant's troops suffered badly and lost a large number of men. Lee lost fewer men in total but a higher percentage of his army. Such arguments can swing one way or the other but the truth may simply be that Grant, by bringing the war to a conclusion – albeit a bloody one – ultimately saved the lives of thousands of men on both sides. On the other hand had Grant not been in full control, Lincoln may well have lost the election to McClellan running on a 'peace platform'. It might have brought the war to an earlier conclusion, but it would most probably also have led to a permanent split between the Union and Confederacy.

Once the war was over, Grant remained commanding general. A few days after the South's surrender, he declined an invitation from Lincoln to accompany him to the theatre. Lincoln was assassinated that night and Vice-President Johnson took over, without great success. In 1869, Grant – who had shown such political astuteness in his behaviour to the vanquished – was persuaded that he, above all others, was the ideal president of reconciliation. He was elected the fifteenth President of the United States. His period of two terms was not outstanding; he successfully trusted his subordinates while fighting but such a policy was less effective in the White House.

In the year before his death Grant wrote his memoirs, which are now generally considered to be one of the finest pieces of American literature. With typical determination, he finished the memoirs days before his death on July 23, 1885.

The Battle of the Wilderness had ushered in a new era in warfare, a taste of what was to come. Grant fully understood the implications of this change, and it is thus as a commander, rather than as president, that he will be remembered.

CHAPTER SIX

GEORGI ZHUKOV

'He was born a military leader. Of the Soviet Generals who so conclusively defeated the armies of Nazi Germany, he was the most brilliant of all.' (Vasilevsky)

The German-Soviet war from 1941 to 1945 was the most destructive in history and left a divided Europe in ruins. Ultimately Nazi Germany was defeated – at an estimated cost of 27 million Soviet lives – and Hitler's reign of terror curtailed. The military commander who deserves the most credit for this victory is Georgi Konstantinovich Zhukov.

Zhukov is as far removed from the Alexandrian ideal of a commander as one could hope to find. This thick-set, stern Russian marshal has little of the charismatic persona that fuelled the Macedonian advance through Persia or the oratorical precision that drove the Roman legions. Nevertheless, Zhukov firmly deserves recognition for having changed world history as a consequence of his command abilities.

Alexander commanded an army of 35,000; Zhukov a force of millions. Alexander answered to no one; Zhukov was deputy to Stalin. Alexander fought to conquer; Zhukov fought to survive. Yet any commander's operational requirements are essentially the same: a clear strategy, efficient logistical supply, fierce determination and overwhelming strength of character. Zhukov was a master of all four.

'Operation Berlin' marked the final phase of the Second World War in Europe. The core of this operation, involving over 2.5 million Soviet troops, was focused first on the Oder River (the Polish-German border) and then on Berlin itself. No city of this size had ever been taken before. It was a campaign that America and Britain, the Soviet Union's allies, avoided, partly for fear of the casualties. But Zhukov and the Soviets did not hesitate or stop until Hitler's proclaimed thousand-year Reich was utterly destroyed.

Zhukov was born on 2 December 1896 in a village about 130 miles (209km) south of Moscow. Russia at this time was under Tsarist rule and the vast majority of rural population, like Zhukov's family, were desperately poor. Nevertheless, the young Georgi

Marshal Georgi Konstantinovich Zhukov at the signing of the final surrender terms in Berlin, 1945.

was able to attend a local school where he showed an early aptitude towards reading and self-education. At the age of ten, however, he was sent to his uncle in Moscow to work as an apprentice furrier.

> Mother gave me some underclothes, a couple of washcloths, and a towel, as well as half a dozen eggs and some pancakes to eat on the way. . . . I saw father's eyes grow red and a couple of tears roll down his cheeks. I could hardly restrain myself, but managed not to cry. (*Zhukov*)

Life in Moscow was unforgiving and the young boy was shown little affection. Childhood was soon over and work meant twelve hours a day for a pitiless master, and sleep on the workshop floor.

The First World War brought escape for Zhukov: in 1915 the nineteen-year-old received his call-up papers and joined the cavalry. Zhukov's natural intelligence marked him out at an early stage and in 1916 he was selected for non-commissioned officer training. His memoirs record that he immediately saw where the problems lay within the Imperial Army. He realized that the overwhelmingly aristocratic generals and officers looked down on their troops and had little understanding or connection with the ordinary soldier. As a result, they were not respected and were sometimes disobeyed. The Russian soldier would fight hard but only for men they trusted.

By the end of the war Zhukov, who had been wounded at one stage, had been decorated for his bravery. But his efforts were largely to no avail because the army

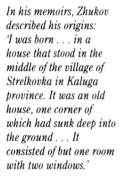

In his memoirs, Zhukov described his origins: 'I was born . . . in a house that stood in the middle of the village of Strelkovka in Kaluga province. It was an old house, one corner of which had sunk deep into the ground . . . It consisted of but one room with two windows.'

Zhukov as an apprentice in Moscow.

collapsed in March 1917 as revolution swept away the old order. Zhukov supported the change and became a member of the fledgling Communist Party. He contracted typhus, however, and returned home and it was not until late 1918 that he returned to what was now called the 'Red Army'.

The first task was to defeat the remaining forces of Tsarist Russia fighting as the White Army. Zhukov once again proved himself to be a bold, competent leader, worthy of the command to which he had been appointed. The Red Army, against the odds, crushed their enemy and the revolution was assured. Much of the army was disbanded but Zhukov, with few prospects in civilian life, elected to remain.

> I arrived at the conclusion that there was no time to waste and that I had to study hard. But my routine kept me busy twelve hours a day. The only way was to add another 3-4 for self education. (*Zhukov*)

While Zhukov studied, Josef Stalin took power and after a brief period of capitalism initiated five-year, then seven-year development plans in order to industrialize the Soviet Union. Stalin's ambition ushered in a period of state brutality rarely equalled in twentieth-century history.

Through determined self-education, Zhukov rose rapidly through the ranks and by the spring of 1923 was commanding a cavalry regiment. Here his character became apparent to all: his attention to detail, his iron will and discipline, his strict-

'Tsarist Regiments and the Red Army' by David Moor, Moscow 1919. Left: 'What they fought for before', right: 'What they fight for now.'

ness of appearance and behaviour. A superior wrote that Zhukov 'loves military matters and constantly improves himself.' Zhukov's potential was obvious and, as well as his command duties, he was also frequently sent on training courses. In 1930, Zhukov became commander of the 2nd Cavalry Brigade and continued to deliver results. He also held seminars, war-games, large-scale manoeuvres, and produced manuals and textbooks. He was particularly keen on experimenting with tanks, though his superiors were convinced these had no role to play.

Highly motivated himself, he had little patience for those who showed slackness or irresponsibility. His reputation as a hard and strict leader of men grew, but he engendered awe rather than fear among his troops. Armies were becoming so huge that without strictly applied discipline and control, the whole edifice could collapse.

In 1937, Stalin began what became known as the 'purges'. He had become paranoid about the potential power of the officer class and decided simply to do away with it. Over 40,000 officers were imprisoned, tortured and killed. Whole strata of the military hierarchy were wiped out. Anyone with a petty rivalry could denounce a colleague. Even three of the five marshals (the highest military rank) were killed, leaving the two who were the weakest militarily, but most politically acceptable.

Zhukov himself was certain he was 'on the list' and indeed always had an emergency bag packed, waiting for the 'knock on the door'. He was not able to relax until 1939 when he made his mark fighting the Japanese.

In June of that year he was sent to Outer Mongolia to report on the situation, as a result of which he was appointed Commander of 1st Soviet Mongolian Army Group. In 1936, the Soviet Union had signed a mutual assistance pact with the Mongolian People's Republic. When the Japanese invaded Mongolia in 1939, the Soviets therefore

Joseph Stalin. Zhukov was one of the few Soviet Marshals to have the courage to challenge Stalin's decisions.

responded. Zhukov was in charge of an immediate three-pronged counter-attack which, because of its suddenness, threw the Japanese back in disorder. The Japanese regrouped on the banks of the River Khalkhin Gol and there seemed to be little the Soviets could do. However, though 400 miles (644km) from the nearest railhead, Zhukov organized a massive delivery of material. By improving roads, reinforcing marshy land, and continuous movement, he managed to assemble a huge tank force. To confuse the enemy, he muffled tank exhausts, constantly redeployed and even left a specially printed pamphlet, 'What the Soviet Soldier needs to know about the Defence', lying around, knowing that somehow the Japanese would get to see one and, when they did, would believe the Soviets were intent on defensive, rather than offensive, measures.

Having prepared the ground, Zhukov unleashed a bitter attack which, in three days, encircled and destroyed the bewildered Japanese. He was rewarded with the title of 'Hero of the Soviet Union'. Thousands of Soviet troops, however, did not survive to be awarded any kind of medal. Zhukov, though not a personally brutal man, saw such casualties as the natural by-product of war:

Zhukov at Khalkhin Gol in Mongolia. Although he was popular with his men, Zhukov was known to be ruthless with subordinate officers who failed to meet his exacting demands.

I made the decision to attack the Japanese with Yakovlev's tank brigade. I knew that without infantry support it would suffer terrible losses, but we deliberately went for it . . . we were prepared for this.

Zhukov's defence was that it was a battle that had to be won. Perhaps he was right; certainly the historical implications are fascinating. Japan saw that the Soviet Union was militarily stronger than it had thought and agreed to sign a non-aggression pact in April 1941. Thus, when war against Germany broke out, the Soviet Union was free to bring troops from the east to fight on its western borders. The Soviets, after the war, believed that it may have been not only the American atom bomb but also – at American insistence – the Soviet rupture of the pact with Japan in 1945, and the subsequent invasion of Japanese lands in China, that caused Japan to surrender.

Meanwhile, war had broken out in Europe. Unlike the relations between Germany, France and Britain, those between Germany and the Soviet Union had always been one of undisguised hatred and fear. The Soviet Union was seen by Germany not only

A German motorised column advancing into the Soviet Union during Operation Barbarossa in July 1941.

as politically dangerous, but as alien and inferior – an attitude encouraged by the German Ministry of Propaganda. The Nazis made it quite clear that they believed all the peoples to the east were subhuman and undeserving of such rich provinces as the Balkans and the Ukraine.

It thus came as a huge surprise to many when, on the 23 August 1939, two such overt enemies signed a Non-Aggression Treaty. But both sides knew the Treaty was a smoke-screen; each had signed to gain a little more time to prepare for an inevitable conflict.

On 18 December 1940, Hitler gave the order to begin planning for 'Operation Barbarossa' – the invasion of the Soviet Union. A vast force of 3.3 million German troops (about the same number as had been fighting on the western front) and 600,000 allies were equipped and prepared for invasion. This was to be a war of total destruction:

> The war will be very different to the fighting in the West. Harshness is a mild word for the future in the East. (*Hitler*)

Zhukov has been called callous but such an accusation must be seen in the light of Nazi atrocities. No war had ever been as brutal as this and the Soviet Union was fighting for its very existence.

In December 1940, Stalin called his high-level officers to the Kremlin for a series of top-secret war-games. Zhukov was in charge of the 'blue' side (representing Germany) and totally out-played his adversaries. Having done so well, he was appointed Chief of the General Staff. An ambitious man, Zhukov had made it to the top. But the task he now faced was much tougher.

First, he had to improve his forces. His soldiers were illiterate peasants, often aware of little more than their own village lives. They had been thrust into a totally new and confusing environment in which they were fighting for survival. There was no question of leave and the norm of daily life was exhaustion, dirt, boredom and extreme anxiety. Only alcohol dulled the knowledge that death was all but certain. These were the men Zhukov had to mould into a fighting force that could defeat the large and excellently-trained German forces. Zhukov worked fifteen-hour days preparing for an imminent German attack. No clear command structure existed; no plans for a defensive reaction or counter-attack had been successfully thought through. There was no defence doctrine, its proponents having been executed for being 'defeatists'. Stalin was fairly sure that they would end up fighting Germany, but he wanted as much time as possible to prepare. He therefore prevented any provocative actions by his officers, though he did allow Zhukov to make a number of secret mobilizations in 1941. Such a strategy meant

Red Army poster, 1941: 'Forward - Victory is at hand!'

that, despite the time gained by the Soviet-German Treaty of 1939, the Red Army was simply not ready when, on 22 June 1941, without a declaration of war, Germany launched a three-pronged attack into Russia.

Stalin and most of the Soviet Union froze. Some soldiers deserted, others panicked. Stalin did not address the population until early July, by which time the Nazis were driving towards Moscow. The German Chief of Staff Halder believed that the Russians had lost the war 'in eight days'.

For the first few months Zhukov tried to plug gaps and raise morale. In September 1941, Stalin sent him to defend Leningrad against a bitter German attack. He replaced the existing commander and staff, and restored confidence, discipline

A dead relative is taken through the streets of Leningrad.

and planning. The city was encircled but not taken. Eventually the Germans, who feared a street-by-street assault, decided simply to let the inhabitants starve to death. Hundreds of thousands did so before the blockade was lifted in January 1944, but the city did not surrender.

Women digging trenches as part of the defenses of Moscow.

Soviet numbers and a fierce determination prevented the Russian front from total collapse. German hopes of a quick victory slipped away as winter approached and a 'Napoleonic' outcome loomed. If only Germany could take Moscow before the snows set in then surely, it was believed with some justification, the Soviet Union would collapse and Hitler would be unchallengeable.

An early problem for the Soviets had been the lack of defensive preparation and planning to counteract German offensives. Zhukov, now in charge of defending Moscow, did his best to strengthen the lines but lacked the troops to do more than cover the main approach routes to the capital. The situation deteriorated to such an extent that classified documents were destroyed in case of defeat. German forces were, however, being drawn off to support actions elsewhere (where Soviet troops were having more success), and the German High Command realized that they were unlikely to

*'Napoleon was defeated.
Just as the upstart
Hitler will be!' Soviet
poster from the defence
of Moscow.*

take Moscow before the winter had set in. They decided to withdraw. The halt to the German advance allowed Zhukov to build up his numbers and launch an attack, which pushed the Germans back across the Volga-Moscow canal. Stalin called for a general offensive which Zhukov felt would be useless without having first accumulated sufficient reserves. Zhukov was overruled and instructed to attack, and despite his best efforts, was soon proved correct. The offensive ground to a halt. Nevertheless, Moscow had been saved, 1,000 tanks captured and 300,000 Germans dead or captured.

Zhukov instinctively knew this was the turning point of the war, but the Germans were far from defeated. In the following summer, 1942, they attempted to gain the upper hand in the south, assaulting Stalingrad in the process, and take control of the coal-mines and oilfields.

In August 1942, Zhukov was appointed Deputy Supreme Commander-in-Chief – the first and only deputy Stalin ever had – and was sent to defend Stalingrad. The city had all but fallen to the Germans, but certain pockets of resistance were holding out and winter was approaching. Stalingrad backs on to the River Volga and across this Zhukov brought a constant flow of supplies. It was dangerous and difficult work crossing the waters and ice of the river but Zhukov and his colleagues never wavered. At the same time, he planned a massive attack against a section of the German line held by Romanians. The operation, effectively a pincer action with a radius of sixty miles (96km), was carefully timed to catch the end of the enemy offensive before it switched to the defensive. The attack was a great success and a further crushing assault on an Italian-held section left the Germans without support. Hitler decreed that it was the duty of the besieged soldiers to die at their posts, and many did. He also made the German commander Paulus a field-marshal because none had

Soviet troops push forward during the vicious counter-offensive for Stalingrad.

ever surrendered. But Paulus gave himself up and broke this tradition. It was a vital victory. Soviet casualties, however, were enormous – perhaps as high as one million. Many thousand are also believed to have been executed for cowardice.

Hitler knew that Soviet victories were often paid for at heavy cost and so, now on the defensive, these heavy casualties were the basis of the calculated policy of the German leadership. By continually conceiving new lines of defence, they aimed to bleed the Soviet enemy to death. The Germans' own losses and military inferiority were of secondary importance. As the Germans retreated they also laid waste to the land through which they passed.

Despite the obstacles, Zhukov kept moving. At Kursk he orchestrated the largest tank battle in history and knocked the Germans back on their heels once again. By March 1944, he had opened up new offensives in western Ukraine, and surging into Poland. By August, Soviet troops had reached the Baltic Sea, and by September they had entered Bucharest, poured through Romania, declared war on Bulgaria and soon reached the River Danube. On 20 October 1944, East Prussia was invaded – now only Poland lay between Zhukov and Germany.

The Soviet assault on Berlin has often been dismissed as a walkover against old men and young boys. But, and this applies to the whole war, events on Germany's western front were very much secondary to those in the east. During 'Operation Berlin' the Soviets incurred casualties of more than 300,000 – as many as the British suffered during the entire war. Berlin was no walkover and the man who led the Soviets to their hard-earned and vital victory, and took the German unconditional surrender, was Marshal Zhukov. Operation Berlin demonstrates the skills that allowed Zhukov to win so many crucial battles and campaigns.

Zhukov's planning, his ruthlessness, as much as his resilience and innovations at the head of the Soviet war machine were, in combination with the Soviet war-machine, simply too much for the semi-broken Nazi regime to resist. Like Grant, he was a commander who understood that he was a mere pawn in a larger political game; his role was simply to do the job asked of him by his superior. The political arena around him was of major importance; Stalin, as well as the Allies, were now fairly confident of defeating Germany and were beginning to ask: what happens after the war? Zhukov had to balance such political considerations against his own military ideas.

The Allies, for their part, were reluctant to storm Berlin. The casualties alone, estimated at 100,000, would almost certainly be politically unacceptable. Why should they fight to get to Berlin when it had already been agreed in 1944 that all this terri-tory (Berlin excluded) would be under Soviet control? In addition, the United States still needed to keep troops available to fight in the Pacific.

The Americans believed, with good reason, that plans were being made to allow Hitler and his close associates to run to the Bavarian Alps. Eisenhower was thus more concerned with sending troops south to cut off that retreat than taking Berlin. Churchill, however, disagreed with such a policy:

Soviet troops advancing into Germany

The idea of neglecting Berlin and leaving it to the Russians to take at a later stage does not appear to me correct. As long as Berlin holds out and withstands a siege in the ruins, as it may easily do, German resistance will be stimulated.

Stalin privately agreed. In the latter half of October, Zhukov was called to Moscow and given command of the 1st Belorussian Army Group. His orders were to get as far west as possible – to the River Elbe, if possible – and take Berlin. Stalin was determined that the prize of Berlin must belong to the Soviets. This was not only a desire for territorial expansion; it was also the understandable wish to enact the maximum punishment on the Germans for the crimes they had perpetrated in the Soviet Union.

Zhukov began work on his plans and by early 1945 he was ready to begin what he declared would be the 'concluding operations of the war'. He decided that there should be a spectacular advance through Poland, moving with such speed that German resistance would crumble. Zhukov put the finishing touches to this scheme and set about organizing the necessary logistical support.

At the end of 1944, Germany surprised the western Allies with an offensive through the Ardennes towards Antwerp. So unprepared were the Allies that the

Americans alone suffered up to 80,000 casualties. Churchill contacted Stalin on 4 January 1945 and beseeched him to make his attack on the River Vistula as soon as possible to draw away German reserves and ease the pressure in the west. This suited Stalin and on 12 January the attack was launched. Within five days Zhukov had taken Warsaw. Churchill thanked Stalin profusely for this success and Stalin later claimed that this attack saved the western allies from defeat.

Zhukov then continued towards the River Oder, the Polish-German border. His forces numbered 2.2 million men (1.5 million soldiers and the rest reserves and ancillary), along a front of over 200 miles (320km). Facing them were about 400,000 Germans, who defended the position bitterly but were forced back in the face of this strength. Zhukov's advance sometimes managed 30-40 miles (48-64km) a day, and his tanks upwards of 60. In total the front moved a remarkable 300 miles (480km) in only twenty days.

By the end of January, the Oder had been reached and in some places crossed. Berlin now lay before them. German defences were not extensive and the city was unprepared. Facing Zhukov were the remains of the German 9th Army, a few groups of disparate troops including a SS reserve battalion, some other small units and home-guard. Zhukov, still flushed with success, initially wanted to continue.

Given four days to replenish his supplies, Zhukov felt he could successfully thrust all the way to the heart of Berlin. However, he had to wait for approval before he could put his plans into action. Stalin was at this time negotiating the future of Europe with Roosevelt and Churchill at Yalta and did not want to be seen to be frantically heading for Berlin. When Stalin eventually approved the advance, Zhukov felt it was too late and ordered the assault postponed.

Having lost the momentum, he now had to act with considerably more caution. He feared that the Germans might break through his northern flank, cut his forces off at the Oder and thus endanger the entire Soviet assault. Zhukov knew that when he resumed the advance he would face much heavier opposition, but he would not move until his supplies were prepared. The speed of his assault though Poland had left his supply lines lagging behind and there were still no railway bridges operating across the River Vistula. Fuel, food, spare parts, ammunition, artillery, transports and reinforcements all had to be drawn up to the front line in preparation for the next onslaught – across the River Oder and on to Berlin itself. Zhukov would not now move until his troops were ready: '. . . to exaggerate the capabilities of one's forces is just as dangerous as to underestimate the strength of the enemy.'

Until the end of 1944, no battles had actually been fought within Germany itself. Except for air-raids the German civilians had escaped the horrors of war. Now the hated and feared Soviet 'hordes' were on the doorstep. Those Germans who knew what their army had done to the Soviet Union had good reason to fear what lay ahead. There was little thought of surrendering, however, and the Soviet pause on the River Oder had allowed the Germans to build up their defences.

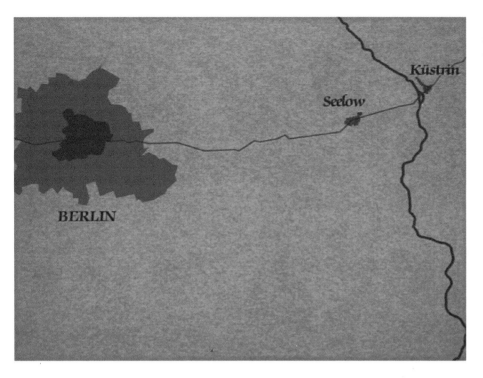

The Seelow Heights dominate the eastern approach to Berlin.

On 2 February the commanders of the German Army Group Vistula were ordered immediately to form a continuous line of defence along the Oder and to repulse all enemy attempts to establish themselves on the western bank. All existing Soviet bridgeheads were to be eliminated. The Germans had used their time to bring this Army Group Vistula up to about 250,000 men (reports vary) but not all were appropriate fighting soldiers: 112,000 men and four parachute divisions had been transferred by the airforce. The navy also sent some Marine infantry divisions who were inadequately trained and lacked fuel, ammunition and equipment. Soldiers, sailors and home-guard had often just stepped off their transports (anything from rail, bus or taxi) when they were marched into position. The best hope lay with the 9th Army, whose numbers had been increased to 200,000.

The first major battle took place at the fortress of Kustrin, an important rail and road junction on the way to Berlin. It lay on the eastern bank of the Oder, and was connected to the German front lines. The civilian population had been evacuated and only 9,000 defenders remained. By the end of March, Kustrin had fallen and Zhukov had secured this important crossing point for the attack on Berlin. The shortest way to Berlin was along Reichsstrasse 1 (Route 1), which went from Kustrin across a demolished bridge through the town of Seelow and on to Berlin. Zhukov intended to concentrate his efforts on Seelow.

Seelow sits on a range of hills overlooking the Oder Valley. The central section of the range, the Seelow Heights, is about 150 feet (46m) high, and, together with the Reitwein Spur, dominates the surrounding marshy area along the river. The Oder

Zhukov and Koniev. Stalin exploited the bitter rivalry between his two marshals during the advance of the Red Army towards Berlin.

Marsh, which had been drained by Frederick the Great, was the area in which the fate of Berlin was to be decided. It stretched 8-10 miles (13-16km) for a length of 45 miles (72km) from Oderburg to Frankfurt-an-der-Oder. The predominantly flat land lies partially below the water level of the Oder and is prone to flooding. In the spring of 1945, the poor condition of the ground, water-logged due to the winter thaw, very much restricted the movement of heavy weapons, particularly the armoured vehicles.

From the Soviet point of view, time was running out by the end of March, especially as news reached Zhukov that the German western front had collapsed and the Allies had reached the Elbe. Stalin angrily declared that Berlin must be taken – and soon.

Stalin feared that the Germans might be able to agree an armistice with the Allies. With hindsight, it seems highly improbable that either Britain or the United States would have agreed to anything but unconditional surrender, but how could Stalin be sure? Hitler had always made it clear that he sought agreement with his opponents in the west so that he could concentrate on the east. The western Allies were clearly less able to sustain and publicly support high casualties and maybe they would contemplate an armistice. Moreover, in 1941, Harry Truman (who became President when

Roosevelt died in 1945) had said in the US Senate that when Germany was winning they should help the Russians and when the Russians were winning they should help the Germans. The Soviets had not forgotten such an offensive remark.

Before dismissing these Soviet fears, one must remember that in February 1945, General Wolff, commander of the SS in Italy, contacted the American Intelligence Service in Switzerland. Wolff was told that any discussions would only be on the basis of unconditional surrender and on 19 March an exploratory meeting was held, to which the Soviets were not invited. Although the British and Americans protested that they had not been concealing anything, this episode only served to further fuel Stalin's anxieties.

On 29 March, the Soviets entered Austria and that same day Zhukov was recalled to Moscow to discuss a plan of operations. Stalin demanded that, as they might be racing the Allies to Berlin, their attack must begin not later than 16 April and finish by 1 May – May Day, the most important day in the Soviet calender.

The plan agreed was that the three main army groups – Zhukov's 1st Belorussian, Marshal Rokossovsky's 2nd Belorussian to the north and Zhukov's arch-rival Koniev's 2 Ukrainian Front to the south – would break through the Oder and envelop Berlin. The main task was Zhukov's: he had to break through the German 9th Army opposite him at Seelow using his main armies and two tank armies: 750,000 men under his personal control (out of the 2.2 million in all) and a great deal of equipment including 1,800 tanks and 3,000 aircraft.

The task facing him was extremely difficult. Even if he managed to pass Seelow he still had to seize Berlin, and no commander had ever taken a city of this size before. Zhukov had to prepare very carefully. He ordered reconnaissance planes to make aerial surveys of Berlin which, with captured documents and prisoner interrogations, were used to compile detailed assault maps. He also had an exact model of the city and its suburbs constructed, which he and his officers divided into the various command sectors.

Although the Germans were outnumbered, they intended to put up a stiff fight. At the most heavily defended position, Seelow, the civilian population had been evacuated, except for adult males who were to remain to build defence positions and fight. The competence of defence building varied but along the Oder there were generally three strips of different depths and levels of fortification. The front line ran near to the river itself and the second line ran along the Seelow Heights. A First World War tactic would be used by the Germans; they would retreat with the bulk of the troops immediately before the Soviets launched their artillery barrage. The troops thus taken from the front line to the second line of defence would avoid the artillery, deceive the opposition as to their position and deployments, waste enemy ammunition and force the enemy to change their method of attack.

The most severe weakness of the German defence was their lack of reserves. This was as apparent to the commander as to the common soldier. Why then did the Germans continue to fight – indeed why did the Wehrmacht (the German army) as a whole not give up? Some still believed fanatically in the Nazi ideals and felt they were worth dying for. Many still had deep fears of the Soviets. Others hoped they could stall the Russians long enough for the Allies to arrive first.

On 14 April, the day after Vienna fell, Zhukov launched a reconnaissance-in-force to gauge the strength of the opposition and clear minefields. This operation was performed by fighting units and a number of German trenches were overrun. The Germans knew they were about to suffer something extraordinary.

Zhukov always thought of new innovations and ideas. They did not always succeed but he never gave up experimenting. From the ruses at Khalkhin Gol to the huge numbers of tanks he fought with at Kursk, Zhukov continually sought new ways to exploit a situation. At Seelow, he organized one of the most intense and terrifying artillery barrages of the war – thirty minutes of non-stop fire supported by an air attack. A clear day turned dark as the air filled with dust and debris. Although much of this barrage landed on the empty front-line trenches, the emotional impact was high: the German defenders on the Seelow Heights were terrified.

Then came the attack. Zhukov ordered that, contrary to normal practice, the attack would take place at night. He arranged for 140 searchlights to be aimed directly at the enemy. These were turned on when the attack was launched. It was an impressive idea but its success is questionable, largely because the Russians failed to take into account the amount of dust and smoke their own artillery barrage would produce. Troops suffered from night blindness and, silhouetted against the lights, were clearly visible. The searchlights themselves were also easy targets, many were hit by German artillery and their predominantly female crews killed.

Zhukov's resilience was central to his success. Nothing could deflect him from his path of aggression against his foe. Seelow was proving bitterly difficult but he would not relax the pressure.

The mined and marshy ground either side of Reichstrasse 1 forced all armoured vehicles to keep to the roads. Many vehicles, especially those that became stuck, were destroyed by German anti-tank defences: 700 tanks were lost in four days. The Germans were so well dug in on, and behind, the Seelow Heights that, gradually, the attack stalled. Zhukov was bitter at the poor results but did not look around to apportion blame on his subordinates: 'Above all, it is I who must shoulder the blame for this short-coming.' (*Zhukov*)

Zhukov was ruthless: he did not believe in the necessity of the personal touch. He expected efficient, dedicated soldiers who wanted to fight through discipline, fear, love of homeland and hatred of the enemy. Cowardliness, shirking and other similar offences were dealt with in such a way as to deter others. There were, for example, a number of officers who, having disappointed Zhukov, were sent to the penal battalions that fought at the most dangerous front lines.

Although things were not going well, Zhukov retained control of the situation. He decided to change his carefully laid plans (which were to commit his two armies after the enemy defences had been breached) and ordered the tanks to intervene and advance up the road. Zhukov was apparently livid with anger at the successful German parrying and this was his response.

The Germans were horrified at the sight of this relentless Soviet advance, an advance that even knocked Soviet troops out of the way. The tanks themselves could not immediately breach the defences either but the decision to deploy them certainly undermined any hopes the defenders had of victory. They knew now that in order to succeed, the Soviets would accept any number of casualties.

By nightfall, Zhukov had still failed to seize Seelow and Stalin now played Zhukov off against his colleague Koniev, operating to the south. Stalin knew that both com-

Artillery, 1944.
Taken by Emmanuel
Yevzerikhin.

manders wanted the prize of taking Berlin and taunted them. He rang Zhukov to tell him that he was now thinking of allowing Koniev to move on Berlin. The ploy certainly worked for Zhukov renewed his fighting with extra vigour. He threw everything he had at Seelow.

Slowly, house by house, Zhukov's troops took control of the streets. A tank corps was also sent north and south of the town, which eventually fell on 18 April. The cost of seizing the Seelow Heights had been high: over 30,000 Soviet soldiers perished here in three days. The losses and the exhausted state of his remaining troops forced Zhukov to revise his plans for taking Berlin.

On 19 April, the 9th Army defence fell apart and the breakthrough to Berlin had been achieved. On hearing the news, Hitler refused to let them retreat. Zhukov simply by-passed them and mopped them up later; they no longer posed a threat as they might have done had they retreated to Berlin and set up a new defensive line.

By 20 April, Zhukov's long-range artillery was near enough to begin pounding Berlin. With tanks and artillery, his armies advanced on Berlin in sweeping movements to overwhelm defenders with shock tactics and superior firepower. Koniev, on the south of the city, had become bogged down and was in need of supplies.

Berlin had been preparing to fight since the end of January. The capital was surrounded by an external no-go area of fortified military bases. The outer defence zone ran roughly along the outer edge of the city following the many canals, rivers and lakes. There was a second line of defence around the inner city, following the S-Bahn (overground railway) ring.

The city had been almost continually bombed by the western Allies since 1943. From the beginning of February, 'thousand-bomber' raids had wrecked the centre of the city, killing thousands of people, many of whom were refugees fleeing both eastern and western fronts. In a total of 363 raids up to 20 April, over 45,000 tons of bombs had been dropped. Zhukov's artillery followed this onslaught with an even greater tonnage.

The civilians and authorities refused to surrender: buildings, in particular the corner houses in command of streets, were fortified. Barricades were erected to cordon off streets, the width of which had already been reduced by mountains of rubble from bombed houses. Trenches, anti-tank ditches and approach trenches furrowed the green spaces and open areas of the inner city as well as the suburbs. The sewers and the underground as well as sections of the S-Bahn were incorporated in to the defence system. Anti-aircraft bunkers, in particular three massive flak-towers with almost impregnable cement walls, also stood ready for the imminent assault.

The Germans lacked the manpower to defend such a metropolis. The core of the city's defence consisted of one tank division and some leftover bits and pieces of other units. Every man in Berlin – whether sixteen or sixty – was drafted in to serve his 'patriotic duty'. The German defence probably amounted to somewhere between 100,000 and 300,000 men. The Soviets, on the other hand, had over 1 million troops advancing on Berlin alone.

A key to the Soviet success in the battle was the army's rapid shift from set-piece battlefield organization to street-by-street fighting force. Zhukov issued detailed orders, which included instructions that 'powerful, destructive groups' be established; heavy artillery, heavy howitzer, and heavy mortar. On the three fronts attacking Germany the Soviets had a total of 41,000 guns and mortars. During certain attacks, these were even positioned wheel-to-wheel, so great were their numbers.

Against such a weight of aggressive force, there was little that the Germans could do to prevent the Soviets seizing Berlin. The Soviets were instructed to push on methodically, each attack preceded by bombs and artillery. Two groups of infantry proceeded along each side of a street, while a third had the job of combing through the buildings behind them. This was done by 'mouseholing' – blowing holes in walls and ceilings and clambering through to adjacent rooms. The infantry was supported by tanks and flame-throwers. Gradually, apartment block by apartment block, shop by shop, factory by factory, the Soviets advanced:

> They enter each house . . . they drive into the gardens with their vehicles and
> tanks, overrun the cared-for garden walls and fences.. (*Rudolf Muller*)

Some troops got lost in the streets, as they could not read the Latin scripted signposts. Others, from outlying parts of the Soviet Union, refused to go below ground into the subways, never having seen anything like them before. Battles raged in the suburbs and the ring around the city closed. During 24 April, units of Zhukov's 1st Belorussian and Koniev's 2nd Ukrainian met. On 25 April, the Soviets and Americans met at the River Elbe.

Hitler decorating German teenagers for single-handed destruction of Soviet tanks.

The storming of the Reichstag building, at the heart of Berlin, was to be the symbol of the Third Reich's defeat at the hands of the Red Army.

In spite of the encirclement, Hitler and his remaining staff utterly misjudged the situation and continued to expect external intervention. They had ordered their 12th Army back from the Elbe, expecting it to come to the aid of the weakened 9th. The 12th, however, full of teenagers, reacted slowly, and did little more than encourage the 9th to make a run for the west.

The Hitler Youth, however, continued to carry out highly successful counter-attacks against the incoming troops. One Soviet commander remembered how at Templehof Airport on 26 April, 400 teenagers equipped with 'Panzerfausts' (shoulder anti-tank weapons) made a short but damaging attack against a tank corps. Hundreds of Soviet tanks were destroyed by boys as young as seven and eight years old.

As Koniev finally crossed the Teltow Canal and moved towards the centre, Stalin divided Berlin in to two seperate fronts, giving his loyal second-in-command Zhukov the prize. Koniev's area of operations ended just short of the target both craved to occupy – the Reichstag. This building had been set on fire by Hitler in 1933, and deliberately left a ruin, but for the Soviets it had great symbolic value, they considered it the German equivalent to their own Kremlin. Heavy fighting continued throughout the city as the Germans were pushed back. Soon only central areas and a strip to the west of the city remained in German hands.

On 28 April, Soviet troops reached the Moltke Bridge, near the Reichstag. The bridge was well defended but Zhukov's imperative was to attack despite the cost and it was indeed taken with great loss of life on both sides. Soviet troops were then able to enter the Ministry of the Interior on the other side of the river. Soon the Soviets were approaching the Reichstag building. To their surprise they suddenly found themselves under attack from the rear (from the Kroll Opera House) and the casualty rate was severe until these German troops were killed and captured.

It took the Soviets four assaults before they could breach the entrance to the virtually indestructible Reichstag building. Flooded tunnel cuttings, mortar and artillery fire, machine guns and mines had all stoutly protected what the Soviets considered the centre of Nazi Germany. As evening fell on 30 April, however, one small group managed to get to the bricked-up main entrances and, by firing at point-blank range through the bricks, were able to scramble inside. There followed a period of confused hand-to-hand fighting in the darkness and dust. But at 10.50 p.m., just before the May Day target set by Stalin, the Red Flag, with its specially large hammer and sickle, was raised on the rear of the Reichstag roof. Bitter fighting carried

The red banner is hoisted above the roof of the Reichstag, May Day 1945.

on within the building until 2 May but the symbolic gesture had been made. (As it was dark it had to be repeated in the morning for the cameras.) Once in control of the Reichstag, Zhukov's troops went on to storm the last bastion of the Nazi regime, the Reich Chancellery itself.

On 30 April, Hitler had asked the commander of the sector how long before the Reich Chancellery – the site of his headquarters – would fall. Twenty-four hours was the reply. That afternoon Hitler killed himself and his aides burnt his body in the garden.

Some of those still present in the bunker, such as Goebbels, Borman and General Krebs, attempted to sue for an armistice. When informed of this by Zhukov, Stalin replied that only unconditional surrender would suffice. Goebbels, after killing his wife and six children, and Krebs committed suicide; others made their escape. Hours later, the Chancellery and its bunker were taken.

> Finally, the goal for which our nation had endured its great sufferings: the complete crushing of Nazi Germany, the smashing of Fascism, the triumph of our cause. (*Zhukov*)

General Weidling, defence commandant of Berlin, surrendered on 2 May, and six days later Zhukov presided over the signing of unconditional surrender at Karlshorst in eastern Berlin. The Germans had signed an unconditional surrender the previous day at Reims, France, but the Soviets refused to accept its validity.

Zhukov had succeeded. It has been said that, given the poor resistance, he could not have failed. But Soviet casualties for the operation are estimated at 300,000 – including 100,000 dead. The Soviets also lost over 2,000 tanks (over half the total), 1,200 guns and mortars and 527 planes; such figures indicate just how hard a battle was fought.

Operation Berlin was the culmination of Zhukov's career but in typical style Stalin took as much of the glory as he could. It is clear how very different the role of a commander in modern warfare had become compared to that of classical times. Zhukov was a pawn in a much larger political game. Stalin wanted to take Berlin and reach the Elbe at any cost, and Zhukov acted according to Stalin's commands. Even though he knew the brutality that Stalin had inflicted on fellow officers, and although Zhukov always feared for his own safety with Stalin, he was a loyal second-in-command. Zhukov put the war against Germany above all else. As a result, he became one of the very few men that Stalin respected and trusted.

Operation Berlin was the first and probably the last battle of its kind to be fought. It involved a major breakthrough battle on a conventional front followed by an encirclement and subjugation of a major city held by a stubborn enemy. To take a capital city – defended house by house, street by street – is perhaps the hardest military objective imaginable, requiring massive deployment of destructive forces. How different Paris would look today if it had suffered a similar assault.

In such circumstances, command and control is extremely difficult. Zhukov could not be sure what he would face and had to plan for all eventualities. The key to Zhukov's command skills was his ability to force his men forward. He achieved this with discipline (there were frequent and harsh court martials), fostering a sense of mission and a feeling of anti-German hatred. Zhukov was forced by political demands to take a city in which even children were fatally dangerous. Had Berlin been better defended, it might have taken months to conquer, but whatever the odds Zhukov would have taken it eventually. Modern warfare requires commanders who can make impossible moral decisions and Zhukov knew he had to do whatever was necessary to succeed. Whatever the obstacle, he would single-mindedly overcome it, whereas lesser men would have wavered. Berlin had to be taken, Hitler's regime had to be rooted out at the core and destroyed, and Zhukov's abilities as a commander saw that it was done.

After the war Zhukov's role was acknowledged briefly. He led the victory parade through Moscow on a white horse and received the crowd's adulation. Stalin was supposed to have ridden the horse but it had thrown him during a dress rehearsal. It

The burnt out shell of the Berlin Reichstag, which became the symbolic focus of the Soviet offensive on the city.

Victory parade in Moscow. Soviet troops throw down the captured standards of the German forces at the feet of the Soviet leadership in Red Square.

was a bad omen. Without warning Stalin made Zhukov an 'un-person'. No other figure would be allowed to eclipse his image as the guiding genius of the war, nor did he want a popular general as a potential rival for power. He refused to have Zhukov killed but sent him off to command remote military districts where he stagnated until Stalin's death in 1953. Zhukov then returned to Moscow and shortly thereafter became Khrushchev's Minister of Defence, playing a role in formulating nuclear pol-

icy. His political career was not a great success – some claimed he was heavy-handed, tactless and arrogant – and he retired in 1957. He was rehabilitated once again in 1965 and appeared at the celebrations to mark the twentieth anniversary of the end of the war. When he died in 1974, he was honoured with burial in the Kremlin wall, but his post-war years had been tinged with sadness due to the fact that he did not receive the recognition due to a great commander.

BIBLIOGRAPHY

Alexander

Adcock, F: *The Greek and Macedonian Art of War* (University of California, 1957)

Arrian: *The Campaigns of Alexander* (Penguin, 1971)

Badian, Ernst: *Studies in Greek and Roman History - Alexander and the Loneliness of Power* (Blackwells, 1964)

Bosworth, A.B.: *Conquest and Empire - The Reign of Alexander the Great* (CUP, 1988)

Burn, A.R.: *Alexander the Great and the Hellinistic Empire* (Widenfeld and Nicholson, 1975)

Connolly, Peter: *Greece and Rome at War* (MacDonald, 1981)

Curtius: *The History of Alexander* (Penguin, 1984)

Errington, R.M.: *A History of Macedonia* (California University Press, 1990)

Fox, Robin Lane: *Alexander the Great* (London, 1973)

Fuller, J.F.C.: *The Generalship of Alexander the Great* (Da Capo, 1980)

Griffith, G.T. (ed): `Views and Controversies about Classical Antiquity' Alexander the Great - The Main Problems* (Barnes and Noble, 1966)

Hammond, N.: *Alexander the Great - King, Commander and Statesman* (Catto and Windus, 1981)

Head, Duncan: *Armies of the Macedonian and Punic Wars* (Wargames Research Group, 1988)

Homer: *The Odyssey* (Penguin, 1972)

Keegan, John: *The Mask of Command* (Cape, 1987)

Lipsius, Frank: *Alexander the Great* (Weidenfeld and Nicholson, 1974)

Plutarch: *Lives Volume VII - Alexander* (Loeb, 1919)

Renault, Mary: *The Nature of Alexander* (Penguin, 1984)

Warry, John: *Alexander 334-323BC* (Osprey, 1991)

Warry, John: *Warfare in the Classical World* (Salamder, 1980)

Wilcken, Ulrich: *Alexander the Great* (Norton, 1967)

Caesar

Barker, Phil: *Armies and Enemies of Imperial Rome* (Wargames Research Group, 1981)

Cicero: *Letters and Writings Volume XXI - De Officiis* (Loeb, 1913)

Connolly, Peter: *Greece and Rome at War* (MacDonald, 1981)

Dodge, Theodore: *Great Captains* (Pallas Armata, 1992)

Fuller, J.F.C.: *Julius Caesar - Man, Soldier, and Tyrant* (Da Capo, 1991)

Grant, Michael: *Juluis Caesar* (McGraw-Hill, 1969)

Grant, Michael: *The Army of the Caesars* (McGraw-Hill, 1969)

Holmes, T. Rice: *Caesar's Conquest of Gaul* (OUP 1931)

James, Simon: *Exploring the World of the Ancient Celts* (Thames and Hudson, 1993)

Julius Caesar: *The Civil War* (Penguin, 1990)

Julius Caesar: *The Conquest of Gaul* (Penguin, 1986)

Needham; C.P.: *Caesar - Politician and Statesman* (Blackwell, 1968)

Plutarch: *Fall of the Roman Republic* (Penguin, 1973)

Polybius: *Rise of the Roman Empire* (Penguin, 1992)

Suetonius: *The Twelve Caesars* (Penguin, 1992)

Watson, G.: *The Roman Soldier* (Thames and Hudson, 1985)

Nelson

Beattie, Dr William: *The Authentic Narrative of the Death of Lord Nelson* (Athemum Press, 1975)

Bradford, Ernle: *Nelson - The Essential Hero* (Grafton, 1979)

Howarth, David and Howarth, Stephen: *Nelson, The Immortal Memory* (Dent, 1988)

James, William: *James's Naval History of Great Britain* (Richard Bentley, 1837)

Lavery, Brian: *Nelson's Navy* (Conway, 1989)

Mahon, A.T.: *The Life of Nelson* (Sampson, Lowe, Marston and Company, 1897)

Masefield, John: *Sea-Life in Nelson's Time* (Sphere, 1972)

Nicolas, Sir Nicholas Harris: *The Dispatches and Letters of Vice-Admiral Lord Viscount Nelson* (Colburn, 1846)

Oman, Carola: *Lord Nelson* (Hodder and Stoughton, 1947)

Pocock, Tom: *The Young Nelson in the Americas* (Collins, 1980)

Pocock, Tom: *Horatio Nelson* (Bodley Head, 1987)

Pope, Dudley: *England Expects* (Weidenfeld and Nicholson, 1959)

Rodger, N.: *The Wooden World - An Anatomy of the Georgian Navy* (Collins, 1986)

Schom, Alan: *Trafalgar* (Joseph, 1990)

Southey, Robert: *The Life of Nelson* (Naval Institute Press, 1990)

Warner, Oliver: *Nelson* (Weidenfeld and Nicholson, 1975)

Napoleon

Chandler, David: *The Campaigns of Napoleon* (Weidenfeld and Nicholson, 1972)

Chandler, David: *The Military Maxims of Napoleon* (Greenhill Books, 1987)

Davout, Louis Nicolas; *Le Marechal Davout* (Paris, 1887)

Duffy, Christopher: *Austerlitz* (Les Coopler, 1977)

Fisher, Hal: *Napoleon* (OUP, 1912)

Francois, Claude and Meneval, Baron N.J.E. de: *Memoirs to Serve for the History of Napoleon I from 1802-1815 (3 Vols)* (Hutchinson and Company, 1894)

Gourgaud, Baron Gaspard: *St Helene Journal inedit 1815 - 1818 (2 Vols)* (Flammarion, 1899)

Henri, Baron Jomini: *Life of Napoleon* (Hudson Kimberley Publishing, 1897)

Jakob, Walter: *A German Conscript with Napoleon* (University of Kansas, 1938)

Les Cases, Emmanuel Comte de: *Memoires de Napoleon* (Maubath, 1818)

Luvaas, Jay: *Clausewitz on Frederick the Great and Napoleon* (US Army War College, 1985)

Maurois, Andre: *Napoleon and His World* (Thames and Hudson 1963)

Grant

Cadwallader, Sylvanus: *Three Years with Grant* (Greenwood Press, 1956)

Catton, Bruce: *Grant Moves South* (Little Brown, 1990)

Fuller, J.F.C.: *The Generalship of US Grant* (Da Capo, 1991)

Frost, L: *US Grant Album* (Seattle, 1966)

Henderson, G.F.R.: *The Science of War* (Longman, Green and Co, 1913)

Lloyd, Lewis: *Captain Sam Grant* (Little Brown, 1991)

Parker, Ezra Knight: *From the Rapidan to the James Under Grant* (Providence, The Society, 1909)

Porter, Horace: *Campaigning with Grant* (Bantam, 1991)

Grant, U.S.: *Personal Memoirs of US Grant* (Da Capo, 1982)

Zhukov

Chaney, Otto P Jnr: *Zhukov - Glasnost and the General* (University of Oklahoma Press, 1993)

Jukes, Geoffrey: *Stalingrad* (Ballatine, 1968)

Knappe, Siegfried: *Soldat* (Orion, 1992)

Le Tissier, Tony: *The Battle for Berlin* (Cape, 1988)

Zhukov, Georgi Konstantinovica: *Memoirs of Marshal Zhukov* (Progress Publishers, 1974)

Miscellaneous

Dixon, Norman F: *On the Psychology of Military Incompetence* (Futura, 1991)

Greveld, Martin van: *Command in War* (Harvard UP, 1985)

Greveld, Martin van: *Supplying War* (CUP, 1977)

Hackett, John: *The Profession of Arms* (Sidgwick and Jackson, 1983)

Holmes, Richard: *Firing Line* (Cape, 1988)

Keegan, John: *The Face of Battle* (Cape, 1976)

Keegan, John: *The Mask of Command* (Cape, 1987)

Machiavelli, Niccolo: *The Art of War* (Da Capo, 1991)

Sun Tzu: *The Art of War* (Shambala, Boston and Shaftesbury, 1988)

Wavell, Archibald: *Soldiers and Soldiering* (Cape, 1953)

INDEX

Page numbers in *italic* refer to illustrations

Picture Acknowledgements

John C Bastias, Ektodike Athenon page: 18; Bridgeman Art Library page: 102; Anne S K Brown Military Collection pages: 104, 105, 113; Otto Chaney pages: 158, 160, 161(above and below), 181; Peter Clayton pages: 10, 22, 59; C M Dixon pages: 20, 25, 29, 39, 42, 57, 58, 68; Mary Evans Picture Library pages: 76, 77, 86-87, 93, 120, 127, 129; Phil Grabsky pages: 6, 8, 15, 31, 34, 38, 43, 46, 50, 51, 52, 63, 65, 67, 69(margin), 70, 79, 83, 89, 100, 106, 107, 108, 110, 111, 115, 119, 126, 150; David King Collection title page and pages: 14, 162, 163, 164, 167, 168, 169, 170, 171, 173, 179, 183, 186; The Mansell Collection pages: 26, 37, 40, 48, 53, 60, 69(above), 71, 81, 124; National Maritime Museum page: 74; Royal Naval Museum, Portsmouth pages: 82, 83, 84, 91, 95, 97, 98; Scala page: 23; Seventh Art pages: 27, 30, 62, 66, 90, 94, 118, 122, 123, 142, 146, 175, 182; US Army pages: 166, 185; US Army Military History Institute pages: 130, 132, 133, 134, 135, 137, 138, 139, 140, 142(margin), 143, 144, 147, 148, 149, 152,153, 154, 156.